A STRIPPED DOWN APPROACH TO INTE

Are you frustrated by modern technology?
Your users are.

Do you wonder why your kids are better at it than you?
Your users do.

Are you responsible for some of the frustrations we all experience every day?
Your users think you are.

Written for software engineers, project and product managers, designers, marketers, CEOs and entrepreneurs, **Taming the Turing Machine** shows why the machine that can do anything has become the machine that does everything. And the machine that does everything has left many of us confused.

In this easy-to-read book, Simon Lewis explores why some digital products are so hard to use, and offers three straightforward but powerful ways to make interacting with them much easier.

Simon Lewis is a software engineer and human being. He's spent much of his life programming computers, and most of it shouting at them. After a decade at HP's research labs developing software for new products like digital cameras, anaesthesia machines, electronic whiteboards and other innovations, he's gone on to work with many other hi-tech companies, always trying to create digital products that are easier-to-use and more enjoyable than most of us ever experience.

Frustrated and embarrassed by the technology industry's inability to design products for ordinary people, Simon has sought to understand human behaviours and motivations, and to deliver products built around them. In his spare time he provides tech support to friends and family who foolishly bought products from companies that didn't share that ambition.

True to his name, Simon spends a lot of time extolling the benefits of simplicity. Not just ease-of-use. Not the anything-but-intuitive interface that every product now claims. But radical, do-less-not-more, what's-really-the-problem-here simplicity. He consults, gives talks, and runs training sessions to share these (simple) ideas.

TAMING

THE

TURING MACHINE

THREE WAYS TO MAKE EVERY DIGITAL PRODUCT USABLE

SIMON LEWIS

First edition published in Great Britain — January 2012

Produced by
Conceptual Simplicity
www.conceptualsimplicity.com

This book is dedicated to Helen, Xander, Imo and all of my family and friends who've ever dared asked me to help make their digital products work, only to be on the receiving end of a rant about why on earth the product wasn't properly designed in the first place.

I'm sorry. Perhaps this will make things better.

Thank you

I only understand the things I'm about to share here because of the **many** talented and generous people I've been lucky enough to work with for over half a lifetime. You're too numerous and varied to name individually, but any of you reading this book will — I hope — know who you are. Thank you for teaching me, learning with me, or letting me try to help you. You share in the insights offered here; the errors, omissions and over-simplifications are mine alone.

Chapter 1

What?

It doesn't have to be this way

I am my family's *techie*. Every family has one. I'm called upon whenever there's a problem with a computer, or anything that works like a computer. These days that might be a mobile phone, a satnav, even a television — computer technology gets into everything now. I'm the person they ask, *"why isn't it working?"*, *"why on earth did it do that?"* or *"will you help me set it up?"*. And I can almost always help. I can often help even when I've never seen or used the product before, and sometimes even over the phone.

So how is it that I can help? And why can't these otherwise intelligent members of my family help themselves? What do I know that they don't? And could I somehow capture and bottle what I know, give it to them, and save myself the trouble of having to help them every time? I wish I could.

Better than that though, could I somehow capture a few design secrets, and share them with the other techies who create these products, so that all these problems wouldn't arise in the first place? Maybe I can do that. It's worth a try anyway. That's what this little book is about. I'm fed up of using poorly-designed and hard-to-use products, and fed up of having to help other people do the same, so I'm trying to make my own life — and yours — a tiny bit easier.

I literally grew up programming computers. For over 25 years I've made my living directly and indirectly by telling computers what to do (and, more often than not, where to go). I spent most of my teenage years and the first half of my career sitting for long hours in front of a keyboard arguing with a wide variety of computers in the obscure languages that techies like me use to tell them what to do (we call it *programming*, of course). I've spent even longer managing and (I hope) trying to inspire teams of people like me, as well as helping others to design and make all sorts of new products that incorporate digital technology.

But all this time I've also been a *user* — someone who simply has to interact with computer-based products every day to get ordinary things done. Like we all do. Over the years, I've become more and more frustrated by the challenges my fellow techies foist onto us users. I seem to be answering more and more technical questions. Things that should be getting simpler are getting more complex, and I don't think it needs to be that way.

I get increasingly annoyed with the things computers and all the products that now incorporate them seem to demand of their users. I get annoyed that these products (and presumably their designers) assume that users have an ever-increasing understanding of the computer world, rather than demonstrating themselves an ever-increasing understanding of the human world. Over time, I've become steadily less interested in the technology, and increasingly more concerned about the poor experience that the technology usually delivers to all of us users.

In my professional life I've read dozens of books about how to design great products, and how to craft *user-interactions* (the technical term for the place where the computer stops and the human starts). I've read lots of other more abstract texts on what the problem is (both technical and organisational), and how to solve it. I'd like to think that over time I've become better at understanding how to design technology-based products that ordinary users can actually use. Or at least, I might be better than the average, which is a good start, but sadly not very hard to achieve (think about that one).

But I've been lucky. I've had the time and been given the space to experiment and learn. The majority of working software engineers, designers, product managers and technology entrepreneurs have no time to work out the things I want to talk about here. They just have to get on with it, cranking out system after system, product after product. And people like me — techies who can help other users to understand, sort out the problems with, and use the products that result — are probably part of the problem. By providing free technical support, we give the designers and creators of these products the excuse they need to make the products the way they are. We pick up the pieces. We hold the other users' hands. We let the poorly-designed products survive and even thrive.

It's time to atone for those sins.

All sorts of ways to make digital products easier-to-use have been suggested. *Point-and-click* interfaces (the sort we all use on our personal computers every day), were once supposed to make things easier — to make computing available to everyone — and for a while they did.

But slowly things got more complicated again. Touchscreens, artificial intelligence, voice-recognition, natural language interfaces, computer-based *agents* and lots of other **technologies** have all been proposed or actually used as ways to simplify the human/computer interface. But they haven't really worked, at least not yet.

There are **organisational** solutions too — bringing new and different expertise into product development teams, and adopting a variety of user-centred design and testing processes. These solutions certainly work, although they also require a commitment to invest in them, and a belief in doing things differently.

But I think there's an easier way. It's not an alternative to those much more sophisticated and insightful processes, and it's not a magic bullet either. It's just some thoughts about what frequently goes wrong when products are hard to use, and what you can do about it.

Over the next few pages I want to share with you just three simple ideas that I've found myself returning to (unconsciously at first, and deliberately later on) over many years of designing, building, and marketing digital products. They are the key ideas (along with a few others) that I expect to continue to champion long into the future in my personal crusade to make life better for us all.

If you look at some of the most successful, easy-to-use, and enjoyable products on the market today, you'll see that they embody these same ideas. They're easy to spot, when you know what to look for, but although many companies and individuals want to emulate the success of these best-in-class products, many just don't know how to do it.

Conversely, when you come across a digital product that's hard-to-use, or if someone else asks for your help to use one of those products, you can almost always pin down the problem you or they are having to one of the three things I want to describe here. Once you've read about them — and I promise it won't take you long — you'll be able to spot their absence everywhere.

Maybe I'm a slow learner, because it's taken me 25 years and lots of effort to understand these three things. Many of the designers of today's digital products don't have that much time, so I hope that I can offer you this understanding in a quick and easy-to-digest way — a way that reproduces as closely as possible the many conversations I've had with the teams and individuals I've tried to help to design better digital products.

This book is for anyone and everyone involved in the creation of digital products. It's for techies, for product managers, designers, marketers, sales and support folks, strategists and CEOs. That's because for truly great products, **everyone** needs to understand and *buy into* the principles I'm going to describe. But it's especially for software engineers. You have your hands on the keyboard and mouse, and you — at the end of the day — often control what gets built and how it works in many projects. The very best products are the result of true teamwork, but all too often the engineers get left alone to get on with it. I want to help you make a great job of everything under your control. And even if you do work in a team where the ways your product interacts with your users are specified and designed by someone else, I want to give you the chance to talk with them on an equal footing, to understand why they might be suggesting certain things, and of course to be able to argue with them properly when they're wrong!

What I'll try to describe over the next 100 or so pages are some simple principles that can help make all digital products easier-to-use. Where appropriate, I've given examples of both good and bad practice, but I've tended to keep these examples to a minimum. I hope that the principles I espouse here are long-lived, but the trouble with examples in the digital domain is that they're often not so timeless. Instead of hard-coding them into the book then, I've set up a website at *www.tamingtheturingmachine.com* that offers more dynamically changeable material. You can also follow events via *@TamingTuring* on Twitter.

Taming the *what?*

Alan Turing was a mathematician who is best known for working at Bletchley Park in the UK during World War II — devising methods and machines to crack the codes used by the Nazis when communicating by radio. He also worked on some of the very earliest electronic computers, and on some of the most fundamental science and maths that underpins all computation.

He introduced and developed the notion of the universal machine — the so-called *Turing Machine* — a simple theoretical computer that is, in principle at least, capable of completing any task that any computer that can ever be built can complete. It's a machine that, if programmed correctly, can do anything that's computable.

The Turing machine is a theoretical idea, through which the science behind computing can be better understood and developed by those who care to do so (not me, I have to say, nor the majority of working software engineers, as distinct from computer scientists). Techies, when asked if a particular computer can do a particular thing, will sometimes reply, *"Well of course it can, it's a Turing machine after all"*.

This idea of a machine that can do anything — a universal machine — is something we'll consider in more detail later. It has brought us tremendous benefits. Its realisation in the form of the modern PC, and a host of other digital products, has literally changed our lives. But it's also brought us almost unlimited complexity. A machine that can do anything will eventually, given enough time, end up as a machine that attempts to do, well, everything.

At its simplest then, this book is about how that complexity arises, what its effects on us are, and what we as technologists can do about it. It is literally, therefore, about *Taming the Turing Machine.*

A note on terminology

Because I know you care, I've tried to be careful and precise about how I describe the things I talk about here. But I don't want to burden you with excess verbiage when it isn't needed, so let me mention a couple of things in advance.

Everything I say here applies equally to both men and women (or girls and boys). Sometimes I'll remind you that that's what I mean by explicitly saying *"he or she"*, or *"him or her"*. But because it gets cumbersome to keep doing that, I won't always do it. I'd like instead to ask you to interpret the occasional *"he"* or *"him"* as being fully inclusive of everyone.

I also use a number of different terms to describe the interaction of humans and machines. I generally (but not always) try to avoid the term *user-interface*, because it smacks of the old-fashioned idea of designing a product (a piece of software, say) and then slapping on an extra layer to *"interface"* it to the poor suckers who have to use it. That's a long way from what we're going to talk about here. Instead I generally like to talk about *interaction design*, because it carries with it more of the idea that the product might have been conceived and designed from the ground up to interact with people. Sometimes I'll use the term *user experience* to describe more generally the idea of how the user experiences the interaction, what he (or she!) gets from it, and how they both feel about it.

One more thing

I've been planning and wanting to write this book for over ten years. Each year that's gone by I've found myself thinking, *"Oh well, it's too late. Technology will soon be universally easy-to-use. The problem will have gone away."* But with only one or two notable exceptions, the problem hasn't gone away, and it isn't too late to make a difference. You can make a difference too.

Before we talk about the details of the approaches I'm proposing though, I'm going to spend a while in the next chapter laying out the problem in more detail, and explaining why we've arrived where we are today. I want to make sure that we've all got the same starting point, and I also want to be sure you're as wound up and frustrated about how bad the problem is as I am. The solution is easy to describe, but not necessarily so easy to commit yourself to doing, so you need to feel passionate about it!

If you honestly think you already feel passionate enough about the problems of hard-to-use digital products, if you already understand how and why they come about, and if covering ground you already know bores you, you have my full permission to skip straight to page 27 now.

OK – everyone else – let's begin.

Chapter 2

Why

How did we get into this mess?

Just 30 years ago, computers were rare and specialised tools. Physically large, they lived in carefully controlled environments, were bought only by corporations, universities, or government departments, and were directly used only by trained specialists. The total number of computers in the world was counted in thousands...

So begin many accounts of the history of computing, and if you've worked in the industry for a while, you may feel you've heard it all before. Now you're worrying that I'll be telling you how computers used punch cards when I started (they did — just about), or how my first computer was a Sinclair ZX80 (it wasn't).

*I promise to share with you soon the key ideas about how we can make digital products simpler and easier to use. Before I do that though, I said I wanted to check that we all agree about what the problem is and how it came about, even if this **is** a story you've heard a thousand times before.*

Listen carefully then, as we explore how the modern world of digital products arose, because you may not have thought of this as the root of the problem we're here to fix. Back to the plot...

The computers of the 70's performed the important data-processing tasks of the day: running payrolls and other accounting jobs; forecasting the weather; simulating nuclear explosions; that sort of thing. Occasionally, and when no-one else was looking, the people responsible for programming and looking after these machines would use them to play simple games.

The idea that ordinary people might want or even need to own computers was considered almost laughable. In fact, the founder of one of the largest computer companies of the day (Ken Olsen of DEC) is often quoted (possibly incorrectly) as saying *"there is no reason for any individual to have a computer in his home"*. But there was.

Now, in the space of a generation, we live in a world that is positively infested with computers. I like that word. **Infested**. Like the insects with which we also share our world, we couldn't live without them, they get everywhere, and their effects are both subtle and substantial. They're also very annoying.

Some of these computers are easily visible to us. They're the desktop machines in our offices, the home computers in our bedrooms, the laptops and tablets in our bags and pockets. We use these incredibly affordable devices for an astonishingly wide variety of things and, at least in the developed world, ownership of more than one personal computer is now very common.

But many more of the computers with whom we share our world are **invisible**. Most of them in fact. They control the engines in our cars, make our mobile phones work, and keep us warm and entertained.

The shear number of these invisible computers is staggering. Think about it — all of these products contain computers as powerful as the room-filling machines of a generation ago:

- Phone (fixed, cordless, mobile)
- Answering machine
- Fax machine
- Radio or television set
- Set-top box
- CD or DVD Player
- TV remote control
- MP3 player
- Digital camera / camcorder
- Printer
- Digital photo frame
- Games console / portable game
- Toys of all sorts
- Baby monitor
- Doppler heart monitor
- Breathing monitor
- Blood pressure / Heart rate monitor
- Blood glucose meter
- Digital thermometer
- Weather station

- Burglar alarm
- Credit card
- Broadband router
- Washing machine / dishwasher / cooker
- GPS navigator
- Mobile hands-free car kit
- Bluetooth headset
- Car radio / TV
- Ticket machine
- Electronic whiteboard
- Language translator

You didn't read to the end of that list did you? You skipped down it because it's just too long. And that's the point. But it's only the beginning. Think of all the invisible computers that run the Internet, and the websites we visit and use many times a day.

We now regard it as normal that if we don't know about something, we *Google* for it. Finding your way in the car is no longer a map-reading problem, but an opportunity to use (and often struggle with) a computer (in that case called a *SatNav*). A whole generation of younger adults can't even remember a time when you couldn't ask a girl out simply by texting her (or sending a message on *Facebook*, or *Skype*, or *Twitter*, or...).

It's a wonderful world for sure, but it has its downside. Just as every day we enjoy the benefits of this revolution (because that's what it is), every day we also suffer the pain it causes. Digitisation makes things harder to use not easier, causes lots of people huge amounts of frustration, and leads to a potential division in the population between those who understand and love technology (and for whom ownership is a pleasure in its own right), and those who simply tolerate or reject it outright — saying in effect, *"it's not for me"*.

All this has happened unbelievably quickly. In some cases the technology we use has developed so fast that we're virtually using prototypes. The industry even has a phrase for this — the *perpetual beta* (named for the so-called *beta* version of a product, the second prototype intended only for early users to try out, explore and report problems with). In other cases, products are developed by designers who simply don't understand how the users of these products really think, and are released onto the market before any real response from users can be incorporated in the design. But, as we shall see, it doesn't have to be this way.

Before we talk about that though, let's ask ourselves again how this revolution came about, because the answer will shed some light on the real problem.

Moore and more

Long before Ken Olsen decided there was no need for home computers, another founder of the computer industry — Gordon Moore of Intel — observed an effect that has since both described and driven the information technology revolution. In 1965 he noticed that the number of transistors on the earliest computer chips, and hence their ability to process information, was doubling every couple of years. Transistors, of course, are the basic building blocks of computers. Like cells in a body, the more of them you have, the more you can do.

This effect, now known as Moore's Law, has continued for over 50 years, and looks set to go on for some time yet. The important thing about this effect is not whether it's precisely a doubling in transistor numbers (it isn't), or whether it happens precisely every two years (it doesn't), but that the number of transistors is being repeatedly **multiplied**, rather than simply **added** to. To remind ourselves why this is important, we need to consider just a tiny bit of maths. I know you know this stuff too, but keep reading.

If you start with a number (any number) and multiply it again and again by another number (even a small one, like two), the result gets very large, very quickly. Mathematicians call this effect geometric or exponential growth. This form of growth is dramatically much faster than the simpler arithmetic growth that we are more used to, where the size, weight or quantity of something grows by a fixed amount added to it each time.

One easy way to appreciate the size of this effect is to consider the story of the rice and the chessboard. There are many variations of this tale, mostly involving a reward requested by an inventor, but which he specified in an unusual and clever way. The reward consisted of a grain of rice placed on the first square of a chessboard, two grains of rice on the second square, four on the third, and so on — doubling the number of grains on each square until all 64 squares are accounted for. It sounds like a simple and modest request. But if it were possible to complete this task, it would require **18,446,744,073,709,551,615** grains of rice (I hope I've got that figure right because I know you're checking it). That's 18 billion billion grains — more than 400 times the reported annual world production of rice. It's this doubling effect, applied every two years over just a few decades, that means today's computer chips contain nearly **two billion** transistors.

It isn't just the number of transistors on a chip that increases this way. The capacity of hard-drives to store information is also increasing exponentially, and the speed of a computer's *clock* has done the same thing. In fact, whereas in almost every other field of engineering a 10% increase in some parameter would be seen as dramatic (using 10% less fuel in your car is a worthwhile saving, for example), the whole computer industry is driven by regular, frequent improvements of at least a factor of two in almost everything. We work in an extraordinary industry that no-one else experiences. It's worth remembering that.

Moore's Law means that the computers we can build get dramatically more powerful every year, year after year. It's as simple as that. But that alone is not enough to cause the proliferation of these machines in our everyday lives — the infestation I talked about earlier. That relies on something else too.

Cheap as chips

The computers of yesteryear were room-filling monoliths consuming vast amounts of power. Luckily though, the changes in technology that have driven up the number of transistors on a chip are actually changes that have driven down their size. These transistors are truly tiny, with sizes measured in nanometres (that's one billionth of a metre). They also consume only tiny amounts of power, although power consumption, the heat it generates, and the battery-life issues that it causes, remain as major hurdles to technology development (battery life is one notable parameter that is not doubling every year). Even so, these physical effects mean we can build ever smaller, ever more powerful devices, year after year.

But even that is nothing new. Exquisitely small and beautifully crafted devices have been around for centuries — think of fine jewellery and Swiss watches. What really matters here is the price. These little computer chips are **ridiculously cheap**. Although the factories that make them are enormously expensive (really hugely so), and the human effort and costs involved in designing them are vast, the resulting products are cheap because they use only small amounts of raw material, require little labour for assembly, and are made in simply enormous quantities. That's why we can almost all own the computers and other digital products that now influence every aspect of our lives.

But Moore's Law, and the transistors it describes, relate to the physical elements of the world of computers — the *hardware*. Even that is only half the story though. Most of the rest of this book is concerned with the other half — the intangible stuff we know as *software*.

The ghost in the machine

Just as hardware developments provide ever more powerful machines on which our computerised devices depend, so software provides the "magic" (or perhaps the curse) through which these machines come alive.

In principle nothing more than a set of instructions for completing a task, we know that in practise software is incredibly complex. It occupies no real space, and yet it grows ever larger over time. Once it's been written by one person or group, it can be re-used and built upon by other people. So just as the power of computer hardware keeps on growing exponentially, computer software keeps on growing cumulatively. With thousands of people working on it over many decades, the amount of software (and the amount of human effort) embodied in a modern digital device can be truly enormous.

Almost all of the behaviour (and misbehaviour) of a computer, electronic product, or anything else that contains a computer is controlled by the way its software works. And yet the cost of that software in production is almost zero. I'll say that again. Software does almost everything and costs almost nothing. Why?

Software is cheap because once it's been **written** (which as a former software engineer I have to admit is not cheap), it costs next to nothing to **duplicate**.

We've seen this effect before. In the fifteenth century, Johannes Gutenberg invented a way of printing books that made them radically cheaper than ever before. Suddenly, many more people and lots of organisations could afford books (initially bibles, but later on lots of different books). Barriers between the few people who could read and the majority who could not were broken down, and the world was changed as a result. There are parallels here with the computer revolution.

So if computer chips get more powerful as quickly as they do, and if they can be made cheaply in enormous numbers, and if the software that makes them come alive can be included for nothing, we have all the ingredients necessary for the mad proliferation of computer technology — the infestation of our world that we've seen happen over the last few years.

Chips with everything

Two hundred years ago, during the industrial revolution, there was a dramatic change in our ability to design and make machines. We also learnt how to control the energy sources on which such machines depended. As a result, there was a huge explosion of mechanization in our ancestors' lives. People feared for their jobs as machines replaced humans, although whole new classes of vocation were also created. New industries, like automobiles and aviation sprang up, and enormous businesses thrived in serving them. Society was changed as a result.

Now, because of the effect of Moore's law, and even more as a result of the economies of mass production, computer technology is getting into everything and replacing mechanization. It is simply much cheaper and easier to use electronics where physical mechanisms would previously have been used. So we now have electronic watches, and electronic controls in our washing machines. Ticket machines are electronic, and we have electronic fuel injection instead of carburettors in our cars.

As well as replacing mechanical devices, this new technology is also replacing humans. When did you last have the pleasure of speaking to a real person on the phone instead of pressing #3 for accounts, #4 for complaints? (I did hear of an automated phone line selling tickets to an Elvis tribute concert where you had to press #1 for the money, #2 for the show... but that's another story.)

And of course digital technology has delivered new industries too. Some of our biggest companies are now computer manufacturers, software companies and mobile phone networks, and who doesn't know someone who works as "something in IT"?

One result of this proliferation, as we've already observed, is that I can now do things that were unimaginable only a decade ago. Who would have imagined that I could look down on my own garden from a satellite, have a hand-held videoconference with someone on the other side of the world, listen to any music I like in seconds, and often do all of this without paying a penny?

But as well as being empowering, this new revolution is also divisive. Many of the things that were once easy-to-use, or easy to do, have become hard. Things that were once easy to understand (like the phone) have become complex. The spread of electronics into every product we touch has delighted some people, alienated others, and at one time or another, frustrated us all. But the real culprit here is not the electronics that's become so powerful, so pervasive, and so cheap, but the **software** that makes it all work. Why might that be?

Man the toolmaker

We grew up in a physical world. Humans evolved to thrive in an environment where our senses — especially our eyes — let us directly perceive the things we interact with. In general, with the notable exception of other human beings, those things were physical, mechanical objects, and our senses provided a real sense of how we were interacting with them, and how they were responding. We'll see why that's important in a minute.

Mechanical objects have two other powerful characteristics though. First, if you're lucky, you can see how they work. This is certainly true for simple mechanisms, shovels, door handles and so on. Second, even if you can't directly see how they work, their complexity is at least constrained by their physical nature. Mechanical things can be only so complex before they become impossible to make, and increased complexity costs real money. That cost is an important limiter of complexity.

But software knows no such limitations. It's invisible, you can't see how it works, and its complexity is all but unconstrained by any law of nature. The result is that electronic products, other products that contain electronics, and anything with software inside, can go on getting more and more complex, almost without limit. This rampant complexity is, I think, why digitisation can so often make these products harder to use, not easier.

Software is also infinitely malleable — or nearly so. It can be made to do almost anything, and yet it is completely intangible, frequently making the experience of interacting with it very impoverished. Software is entirely artificial. The interfaces it presents to the outside world — to the humans who must use it — have to be artificially created (often badly). They don't just naturally exist as is so often the case with mechanical objects.

Again, perhaps as a result of our evolutionary heritage, humans learn mechanical skills very well. It's not hard for many people to become very proficient at driving a car, for example. This mechanical proficiency even applies when it comes to some forms of interaction with electronic devices — typing on a keyboard for example, or even entering text into a mobile phone.

But it's a different story when it comes to the abstract world created by software. We didn't evolve to handle such environments where nothing is tangible, and physical laws don't apply. Anything can happen in such worlds, and frequently does. It's a wonder, in fact, that we can reason at all about — and eventually even feel comfortable with — some of the concepts we now have to deal with as we interact with information technology.

As this proliferation continues, I worry that a process of feedback ensues. Computers get more and more powerful, but our brains stay the same. The few people who do understand the technology soon become the people who design it. And unfortunately, they often design it for other people like themselves. The people who don't understand technology become slowly more disenfranchised, and a divide emerges between those who understand and love technology, and those who don't.

This divide mirrors what was once the case with reading and writing — even to the extent that we refer to and sometimes attempt to teach something called *computer literacy*. But what a silly idea that is. We should be encouraging our designers and engineers to understand humans instead. The computers that infest our world are guests here. Like good guests they should learn how to behave, and not require us to adapt our behaviour or the ways we think to accommodate them. We should be teaching our computers, and the people who design them, *human literacy*. That's what I'd like to do.

What's it doing now?

The label in the photo below was wrapped around a digital product I bought a few years ago. The product was from a well-respected multinational manufacturer, and was marketed as delivering the benefits of what it did to a broad audience of non-techies. In fact, its very reason for existing was its purported ease-of-use compared with the competition at the time. That was its claim to fame, it's unique selling point, and yet the experience of using the product began like this, with the product's designers admitting that their users would have **no chance** (their exact words, in bold, as you can see), no chance of using it without first reading the manual. I was speechless when I saw it, as I hope you are now.

IMPORTANT

YOU HAVE **NO CHANCE** OF OPERATING THIS UNIT UNLESS YOU REFER TO THE USER INSTRUCTION BOOK.

In particular, before using this unit, you **MUST** carry out the *Installation* and *Registration* procedures in the User Instruction Book.

This unit will not work until Installation and Registration have been completed.

PULL TABS TO REMOVE

Being able to understand something depends mostly on it being predictable. That's the real meaning of that abused word *intuitive* (which these days often means anything but). If you can't predict what something will do and how it will behave, you can't understand it. You have to read the manual instead. It's as simple as that. It applies to humans (think how hard it is to work with someone who is unpredictable). It applies to the physical world we've evolved in, where centuries of scientific understanding depend on the idea that there are laws that are always the same and that they are the same everywhere. And it applies to the machines we design.

That's why us techies understand how to use technology — because we understand how it works **inside**. We understand the patterns of behaviour that the technology exhibits, however strange they might be to the uninitiated. It might also be why children find technology easier to use than adults — because looking for and assimilating patterns of behaviour is what children do best. But those patterns are not patterns that ordinary people are used to.

For everyone else, the difficulties of using most digital products just keep growing. Yes, there are one or two notable exceptions — a few, very rare, designers who have "cracked it" and worked out how to create delightful and usable technology. But most technology still works in mysterious ways, and those few people who understand it often end up designing more of it. All too often, us techies unconsciously design for *"people like us"*. But most users aren't like us. Eventually, the complexity that results from this way of creating technology becomes over-whelming, and even those of us who claim to understand it become more and more frustrated by it (I do, and I am — ask my wife).

As one final indication of how dramatic this 30-year journey has been, consider the often re-told (and of course apocryphal) story of what our cars would be like today if they'd experienced the same rate of change as computer technology has. They would, it's said, get 1000 miles-per-gallon, travel at 1000 miles-per-hour, and yet cost only £25. Whether true or not, the equally apocryphal repost is even more telling. These modern cars would also, apparently, require rebooting every time you got lost, need their engines completely re-installing whenever something minor went wrong, and would crash twice a day for no reason.

And yet miraculously, cars have actually got better over this time. Despite all the computer technology they contain, they're so much simpler to own and use than they were 30 years ago. You just put fuel in at one end, and drive them at the other. Why can't computers and other digital information products be like that?

I believe they can. It's perfectly possible to create products that do not need an instruction book, much less require their users to read that book before having **any chance** of correctly operating the product. But to many creators of digital products, how to achieve that result seems to be a mystery.

One last time — it doesn't have to be this way. I hope we now agree on what the problem is. Let's start to unravel the mystery of how to solve it.

Here's the secret

In the rest of this book I'd like to share with you three simple thoughts. Yes, I'm going to suggest that there are three ways that all digital products could be designed to make them easier-to-use, more enjoyable, and (I'll stick my neck out here), more likely to be commercially successful. I'll show you how to take these things into account if you're the designer of a new digital product, and how to recognise these things if you're a user choosing which product to buy. And remember that when I say *product*, I actually mean

anything that's controlled by digital technology, whether it's really a computer, a device like a camera or a ticket machine, or a service offered over the web, the phone, or any other digital medium.

The three things to do are:

1. Reduce the **number of features** the product has;

2. Introduce a strong **mental model**;

3. Pay attention to **aesthetics.**

Each of these things has a separate benefit, but they also interact very strongly. We're going to talk about each of them separately in the next three chapters, but it's always best if you actually do all of them, and do them in the order they appear above (and in which we'll talk about them).

I'm not, of course, claiming that these principles are a panacea — that they're they only things you'll ever need to do to make every digital product you create wildly successful. That's far from true, and the extensive body of knowledge and books on product management, marketing and interaction design in all their true sophistication illustrates that fact.

To help explain where the three things we're going to talk about fit into the big picture of what we might call *the user experience*, I've represented them in the diagram below as the three dark-shaded boxes.

User experience

Ease of use

Simplicity

Mental models

Aesthetics

(and other things)

User value

- What problem it solves
- What benefits it offers
- Why I need it
- Why I want it
- How much it costs
- What it says about me
- (and other things)

- How I find out about it
- How it works with my other things
- How I get and receive and service

- How I buy it
- How it's supplied
- (and other things)

You can now see, for example, that I don't intend to talk at all about the things that might make a digital product actually **useful** as opposed to merely **useable**, because that's a completely different story that I'll leave for another time. Neither am I going to talk about the **process** of designing user-interactions, or about how to **test** and improve your efforts with real users, or about the plethora of other things that influence whether people want to buy your product, and whether they're glad they did if they do so. You'll need to look elsewhere to learn about those things.

Instead, what I'm going to offer you here are just some simple but key considerations that I think are missing from the vast majority of digital products we all use every day.

These are the things that I've been worrying about and doing over 25 years of designing, building and selling digital products, and which I plan to continue to champion long into the future.

These things are not novel. Not all products are missing them. In fact, they're well understood and regarded as *received wisdom* by the top designers of successful products. But too many of the designers of the products we all use day after day are repeatedly and quite systematically doing the opposite things, and then presumably wondering why their products haven't achieved their goals (because everyone has "easy-to-use" as a product goal, don't they?).

Neither do we, as users, always understand that these are the characteristics that make the best products easy-to-use. These are the characteristics that delight us, and make us recommend products to our friends. These are the things users should be demanding, and that designers should be offering. These are the things we should be rewarding the best companies for. I know you want to emulate the success of these best-in-class companies, and I'd like to show you how you might be able to do just that.

All right? Let's begin with the first idea — reducing the number of features in the product. Something I call *simplicity*.

Chapter 3

Simplicity
Why less really is more

At the end of the last chapter I revealed the three things that I think could help make every digital product better, and which I claim are already doing just that in the very best products and services. In the chapter after this one we'll get to the heart of the matter and talk about one of the most over-used words in the technology industry: *intuitive* — a word that by its very utterance is supposed to confer an almost magical usability on any product or service that it describes. But here, in this chapter, I'd like to set the scene by tackling perhaps **the** most over-used word in the industry. It's a little word that hides some surprising subtly, but I want to show you that with the right approach, it can live up to its name: *simplicity*.

   Simplicity comes in many forms, and it's easy to get confused and distracted by the distinctions between potentially quite different ideas like *simple-to-understand*, *simple-to-use*, and even *simple-to-learn*. Instead, I want to convince you that there is only one type of simplicity that really counts: **doing less.**

Making your product do less is the first and most important step towards making it easier to use. It's an idea that the technology industry has extraordinary difficulty with, and yet it's one of the most powerful, if counter-intuitive ways to make products better. Even more importantly, reducing the number of things your product does actually makes the other two ideas we'll talk about later much easier to do as well. So it's a double win, and it's therefore important to consider and to do it **first.**

What's the problem?

As we've already seen (and it's a topic we'll return to again), most features in a digital product are cheap, at least once they're implemented. It doesn't cost much to offer lots and lots of features in a manufactured product. It's also easy to believe that your product is more likely to be what the user wants if you put plenty of features into it. So having more features can seem like a cost-effective way to beat the competition at their own game, and putting in lots of what customers want is always a good idea, isn't it? So what's the problem again?

The problem is that having lots of features, although it seems like such an attractive thing to do, almost always makes a product **harder to use**, and potentially **less effective** at what it does. So although your product might be "better" because it has more features, it is quite likely to be "worse" because it's harder to use. That might not seem obvious, so to understand why it might be true, let's draw on an analogy from the world of physical things. It's an oldie, but a goodie, so indulge me once again while I tell you another story.

That's not a knife

Think of the *Swiss Army knife*. Like many gadget fans, I love Swiss Army knives. When I first left home to go to college I bought myself the top-of-the-range, largest, most feature-packed knife money could buy. *The Champ*, I think it was called, and it had **everything**. I still have it in fact, 30 years later. Occasionally, I take it out of the bedroom drawer that I keep it in and admire it. It's in perfect condition — a beautiful work of art. But I never use it. And here it is — the very one:

In contrast to my near-pristine Swiss army knife, many of the simpler tools I've bought over the years are really showing their age. I'd like to think they're just as good quality, because I don't believe in buying tat. Instead, the real difference is that they've been used. They've been used because although they only do one thing, they do it really well and they're (mostly) very easy-to-use.

And that's the point. When a product has lots of features, they inevitably interact with each other, and the result is not always pleasant. All the blades in my knife have to fit together into the same handle. That means that their individual design is compromised. They simply can't be designed with the same singularity of purpose as a stand-alone knife, a screwdriver or pair of scissors. So I don't use them.

Now, this argument has been offered in the past to make the case that digital products should only do **one** thing. One thing per product, done really well, just like conventional (physical) tools. I'm **not** making that case here. Some wildly successful products do lots of things — although usually only one at a time. The most obvious example as I'm writing this is the smart phone, and its close cousin, the tablet. But I would argue that these products are actually great containers for multiple individual "products" that today we call *apps*. Each of these apps – the best ones anyway – adhere to my *"offer fewer features"* guideline. So much so, in fact, that we'll return to this example shortly.

What I **am** saying here is that if you try to jam too many features into one product (including into one app), there comes a point where even though they fit, technologically, you begin to strangle yourself (and your user) when you try to make them fit logically. There are too many of them, and they may not even belong or get along together.

There's another problem too – and it's a big one. On the rare occasions when I might use my Swiss Army knife I can never find what I'm looking for. I know there's a wood saw in there somewhere, but if I ever needed it (which I don't think I ever have because I have proper saws for sawing wood, but anyway, if I did), I'd probably have to open up half a dozen blades before I found the right one.

Sure enough, one of the big problems users have with digital products is **navigation**. They get lost trying to find the feature or function they're looking for. The next chapter on mental models offers a real solution to this, but why make life harder than you need to by having so many features? When you add extra features to a product, you make the most important features — the ones everyone needs every day — much harder-to-use simply because you risk making them much harder-to-find. Where is the mute button on the TV remote control below, for example? It's there somewhere, but where?

The best digital products (as we'll see in the next chapter) allow their users to build a mental *map* of the territory, to understand easily where everything is and how to get to it. When there are too many features, it becomes much harder for the designer to come up with a good way to categorise everything, so the user never builds a good mental map of where everything is. They just have to hunt around every time they need a feature that they know is in there somewhere. You've done that, haven't you? In fact, the situation has become so bad in some cases that the most complex software products now even provide a search function that works not just over your own content (your files and what's in them) but over the features of the product itself. You can search for the name of a command and the system will show you where it is in the menu structure. It's actually very useful, but it shouldn't be needed!

So, over the next few pages, I want to persuade you that you can make your product **better** by making it do **fewer things** in carefully chosen ways. Your users will thank you for it, believe me. But even if you're already convinced that you want to give your product a bit of a pruning, you may be finding yourself fighting a battle to get everyone else in your team to agree. In that case, I want also to offer you the support you're going to need to persuade your colleagues to cut out some (or even most) of your product's features, because it's never an easy thing for everyone to agree to do.

A word of warning

At this point, some of you will be thinking, *"Ah yes, but I can have my cake and eat it. Instead of getting rid of extra features, I can hide them under a physical flap, or behind an* **Advanced...** *button, or otherwise design things cleverly so that different features progressively reveal themselves only when needed by my product's power users."* And yes, you can do that, but I'd like to suggest a couple of strong caveats.

First, you might not be clever enough to really hide the right things in the right way so that they don't upset most users but are available to the few who need them. It's not at all easy to do. You're really replacing one design problem (too many features) with another (how to hide and reveal them). If you're not careful, it can easily become the digital equivalent of hiding all your excess belongings under the bed. It's not as good a solution as properly getting rid of them completely.

Second, even a naïve user (or just someone else who might have used the product before him) will often be tempted to have a little look under the bed. What will happen then is that he'll turn on some mode or other, go back to what he was doing earlier, and then several days later wonder why the product is doing strange things for no apparent reason. He'll end up asking the question I asked in the last chapter (and that I'll tell you how to avoid in the next) — *"why on earth is it doing that?"*. He might then, if he's clever, start Googling the many web forums that most widespread products spawn to allow slightly more expert users to help slightly less expert users with problems like this. He might also call on the services of his local friendly techie (isn't that where we came in?). What he **won't** necessarily do is to guess that the cause of the problem is a hidden setting he fiddled with days or weeks previously. But he shouldn't have to do any of these things, because the real cause of the problem, the underlying issue, the original failure, is that someone wasn't brave enough to make the decision to put in **fewer** features, or get rid of the option that the user ended up accidently setting.

For these reasons, I encourage you to treat the idea of *layering* a user interface, and the notion of progressively revealing its features, as sophisticated approaches of last resort. Or at the very least, regard them as sophisticated approaches of second resort, to be used only once you have ruthlessly pruned away as many features as you can, and followed the advice in the rest of this book. Don't use them as an excuse to ignore this chapter and keep putting in as many features as you like. Instead, simplify, simplify, simplify.

As simple as possible, but no simpler

Although I'm suggesting to you that you can make your new digital product better by making it do less, it turns out that removing extraneous features, caveats and design details is not a new or unusual idea. For centuries, philosophers, architects, designers, scientists and others have expounded, explained and justified the idea that *"less is more"*.

Einstein, for example, is credited by many with the notion that a scientific theory should be as simple as possible (but importantly, no simpler). The concept of *Occam's Razor* is a much older exhortation that we should prefer simpler explanations (meaning less complex, rather than necessarily easier-to-understand) over more complicated theories — everything else being equal.

Meanwhile, in art and design, the term *Minimalism* has been used to describe the various different groups and movements who have reduced their work to the very essence of the thing, the better to see what it actually is, what it really means, or how it works.

In the world of movies, television and video, the skill of editing is very often the skill of knowing **what to leave out**. It's about knowing how to tell an epic story in just two and half hours. It's about knowing how to show just enough of something that our imaginations fill in the rest.

And in the modern world of business jargon, we are often exhorted to *"Keep It Simple, Stupid"* (KISS), by people who know what they want, even if they don't always know how to achieve it. See? We're in good company.

So if making something better by making it do less is such an effective strategy (or would be if more people did it), why are so many digital products so complex? Why are our lives being made unnecessarily miserable by products that have far too many ill-conceived features? Why doesn't everybody already just aggressively prune the list of features in their product? Why is the technology industry different from everywhere else?

I think there are three main reasons why this process of

product editing doesn't happen nearly as much as it should. Let's consider each of them in turn, and talk about what you might do to combat them if you decide that pruning your product is the right thing to do.

The terrible Turing machine

The first reason that digital products have too many features is simply because they can. As we've seen, the computer is a unique invention. No other machine behaves in quite the same way. Most machines do either one thing or a fixed set of very similar things. They do the things they were originally intended to do by their designers, and nothing more. They are the tools that help us do things we couldn't otherwise do, at least not so well. Things like open tin cans, weave cloth, fly to the moon. Those sorts of things.

Just like those other tools, a computer does only one thing. It follows a set of instructions. Without instructions — without software — a computer does nothing. It just sits there. But unlike other machines — unlike other tools — once it's programmed with the right software, a computer can do literally any information-processing task. It is in that sense a **universal machine** — a machine that can do **anything**. And I'd like to suggest that it's therefore unfortunately also a machine that can do **everything** and all too often does just that.

Computers of all sorts are now so commonplace that it's difficult to appreciate how fundamental and important this idea of a universal machine is. In the 1930s, the mathematician Alan Turing was able to prove that a very simple computer is capable (given enough time) of completing any computable task. This idealised computer has become known as the *Turing Machine*, and it's from that idea that this book takes its title. Since all modern computers are functionally equivalent to a Turing Machine, all modern computers are also provably capable of completing any computable task.

This idea of the Turing Machine — the universal computer — has a profound impact on the capabilities of software, and on the creation of every digital product or service. The effect is familiar to anyone who uses a modern digital product. Because the computer inside can do **anything**, the creators of its software are irresistibly tempted to make it do **everything**. And so it does.

As we saw in the last chapter, computing hardware has become extraordinarily cheap, and it goes on getting cheaper all the time. This means that computers continually get faster and have more memory for no extra cost. That's why feature after feature can be added to every piece of software without any real penalty (except of course, as I'm suggesting, to the poor user). As more software is created, so the computer power goes up to be able to run it. As computer power goes up, so more software is created to use it. The industry even has a term for this: *bloatware* — applications that are so loaded with features that they actually become less usable rather than more useful.

I once worked on a project where one of my fellow engineers suggested that it was very wasteful for the computer power inside the product not to be fully used all the time. It was as if he was suggesting that the processor inside every microwave oven would get bored if it wasn't cooking a gourmet dish and simultaneously forecasting the weather instead of merely warming up some leftover pizza. Perhaps that kind of thinking is what results in all the buttons and impenetrable modes that most microwaves seem to sprout instead of just the three controls that are all we really need (power-level, timer, start/stop). In a later chapter I want to suggest a better use for all this computer power, but for now let's get over feeling guilty about the possibility of machines experiencing boredom, and just let them relax and **do less**.

Think about it another way. In the real world of physical products every extra feature takes up space, introduces mechanical complexity, potentially affects reliability, and certainly increases material and manufacturing cost. So there is a real calculable business incentive to be ruthless and keep surplus features out. That's why Swiss Army Knives are so damn expensive compared to real ordinary screwdrivers.

But in the software world, there are no such tiresome restrictions. The product can be "improved" by adding features without violating any fundamental law of the universe. Although it costs money, effort and time during the design and testing phase, once the product is in production, the extra features are almost free. Features get added simply because they **can** be added, and **might** be needed. And it's better to be safe than sorry, right? Wrong.

I want to persuade you to resist that temptation to add extra features just because you can. One way to do this is to ask yourself, *"Would I include this feature if it was a physical product?"*. It's oh-so-tempting to think that adding a feature only costs something at design, implementation and testing time. After that it's free isn't it? No it isn't.

It might be free to you, the manufacturer, but it costs your poor user extra mental anguish every single time they use your product if it's full of features they don't need, but which get in the way of their understanding of the few features they really want, and of what your product does and how to use it. That's the real cost of those extra features you thought could be included for free, and that's what you should be trying to avoid.

Poor product management

The second reason that digital products have too many features is indecision. All to often, nobody knows clearly enough what the product is for, or more commonly too many people have subtly or drastically conflicting views on what it should do. Again, because the cost of offering extra features is so low, the easy way out of this problem is to put in lots of different features just to be sure. *"Let's make it do everything, and then something's bound to stick."*

I'm writing this on a computer. I could be using a simple pen or a pencil, but I'm using a word processor that has literally hundreds of different features. It has probably every feature that every customer has ever asked for, and then a few more that they didn't ask for but which the product designers thought they might ask for, and a few more that someone else thought were just *"neat"*. It's what the computer industry calls *feature-rich*. In fact, it has so many features that it has to have the additional feature of letting me decide which features I want to have on my toolbars and where. It's almost as if the designers and engineers got so overwhelmed trying to tame the complexity that they'd created that they've given up and said to their users (me and you), *"Here you go, we've had enough. You decide what you want"*.

And I do. As a youngster I had a copy of a book called *Scouting for Boys*. One of the pieces of advice I remember it containing was this: *"When you come back from a camping trip, sort your equipment into three piles – things you used frequently; things you used occasionally; and things you never used. If you want to travel light, take only the first pile next time you go"*. I've never enjoyed camping, but that advice has become one of my mantras for good digital product design.

Every time I get a new piece of software (or, heaven-forbid, a whole new computer) I spend a lot of time using the *Preferences* feature (or whatever equivalent is available) to **turn off** every bell and whistle, and to strip out every button I don't need, the better to see the few features I use all the time. I get rid of all that excess stuff the product's designers put in, or allowed to stay in because they didn't have the vision, clarity or gumption to take it out.

The trouble is, most users aren't like me. They don't have the time or the inclination to finish the designer's job.

They just have to put up with the mess, and suffer the difficulty-of-use that results. They live their lives with tool bars that take up a huge proportion of the space on their screens that should be available for their content, and they persist with desktops covered in extra free software that came with their PCs.

Now this isn't a book about product management. There are plenty of other, better texts that you can read to learn how to understand what your market wants, and how to develop a specification for a roadmap of products that might deliver it. What I want to do here though is to persuade you to stop and think hard whenever you find yourself struggling to decide which way a feature should work, or which of two features should be included in a product. If at that point you are tempted to give the user a choice (perhaps via some kind of configuration setting somewhere), or to include both features just in case, please stop again and ask yourself if that's really the right thing to do.

Yes, of course there may be a few users who will be disappointed that you didn't offer an obscure way to present their data, or to arrange their folders in a window, or something else. You may even be one of those "power" users yourself. So might the people around you. But remember the important maxim we'll come to in more detail in the next chapter: **the user is not you.**

Every time you give your user an extra feature, you're potentially adding to his burden as a user, and failing to deliver on yours as a designer. Unless that feature is positively part of the value your product offers it's often a burden your user could do without. Just as it is on a restaurant menu, too much choice is a bad thing in a product. It obscures good design, and wrecks usability.

Feature richness

Perhaps because it's so easy (and cheap) to do, and because it feels like the right (or a safe) thing to do, the third reason I think digital products have so many features is simply because that's the way the industry works. Many people (but not the majority of users, I'd suggest) like it that way. It's a competitive world, and the competition is all too often played out in terms of who has the most features. *"You've got 50 features, so I'll have 60". "I'll make my TV set be a digital photo-frame and a web-browser"*. Marketers, sellers and even some of the more techie buyers of digital products have become used to comparing the length of the feature-list. In their opinion, the more features the product has, the better it must be, even to the detriment of usability.

For long-lived products, this process of adding new features goes on year-after-year, with each new version of the product having to incorporate new features whilst retaining all the old *legacy* features in case someone somewhere is actually using them. In the commercial world at least, it's rare to see features *deprecated*, or flagged for removal from later versions of the product. Curiously though, when software engineers create products for themselves (programming languages, for example), they are often much more aggressive about removing such "cruft". It's strange but true.

Breaking this feature-list-driven approach to product design takes real nerve, but there's recently been an interesting crucible from which has emerged some nice examples of the benefits on offer for doing just that. It's time to return to the fascinating story of smart phones and tablets.

Smart phones have much less computing power than desktop or laptop computers. They have less screen real estate, and less memory too. Of course, they still have a lot more *oomph* than many other digital products, but it's the **contrast** between smart phones and personal computers that matters here.

Many companies who've built their businesses on the back of feature-rich websites have, over the last few years, complemented those websites with app versions of their offerings. I'm thinking of successful companies and ventures like *Amazon*, *eBay*, *Facebook* and *Twitter*. The relatively constrained computing and interaction environment of a smart phone has meant that the designers of these apps have presumably had to make some tough choices about which features to include and which to leave out. The positive result, I'd suggest, is that these app versions of *Amazon*, *eBay* and the others are actually in some ways **better** than the main websites. I certainly sometimes find myself using them in preference to the main websites, even when I have both available.

Now some of this betterness is down to the portable, always-available, instant-on characteristics of the smart phone. But some of it, I think, is down to the ruthless editing, the pruning back that's had to go on to convert these sometimes hugely overgrown websites into a lightweight and **usable** app.

More than that, the invention of the app as a concept — as a deliberately tight and atomic piece of functionality — has unleashed a wave of creativity and value from the software industry. It's as if the industry suddenly got brave about leaving things out.

And that should be an encouragement to anyone who wants to put fewer features into their product, but is afraid the market won't accept it. Try thinking of your product as an app even if it's not, and see if that helps both to focus your mind, and to let you believe that more successful products really can have fewer features.

If that doesn't work, and you find yourself (or your colleagues) still irresistibly drawn towards the comfort blanket of ever more features, remember that **usability** is the one feature that everybody wants. With the exception of a few very special cases (like games), nobody (except perhaps the competition) wants your product to be hard-to-use.

But usability is **not** a simple feature you can bolt on to a huge pile of other features. Because ease of navigation is such an important contributor to usability, better usability is very often about having fewer features. The fewer features you have in your product, the more usable it will generally be. In fact, I like to remember a simple equation that is almost always true:

feature-rich = usability-poor

I hope that the next time you hear someone else use the expression *"feature-rich"*, you'll automatically ask yourself (and them) the question *"does that mean usability-poor?"*.

If in doubt, leave it out

And so we come back to what I believe is the first and most effective way to deal with complexity and to *Tame the Turing Machine*. The first way to make your product easier for your users to use is simply this:

Offer fewer features.

If the first version of your product does the most compelling and important things that users are actually buying it for, if it solves the pressing problem they have, or if it delivers new and exciting possibilities for them, that's enough. If it doesn't do any of those things, no amount of extra features will make up for that basic omission.

Then, over time, as it becomes clear that they are **necessary** (or at least, **desired** by a large number of your real-world paying customers), you can add extra features to your product. That, after all, is one of the great delights (and as we now know, problems) of the digital world — the ease with which you can add new features, even after you've sold the product in many cases.

What you will never do (or very, very rarely) is to take features **out** after you've launched your product. That almost never happens except in the most enlightened and progressive environments. So if you include extra features in your product willy-nilly, and it turns out they're not needed (as they almost certainly won't be), you and your users are likely to be stuck with them for ever, cluttering up and damaging the user-experience of your product, for an equally long time. And you wouldn't want that, would you? I know I wouldn't. Not as a designer, not as an engineer, and certainly not as a user.

Summary

Over the last twenty or so pages, I've tried to persuade you that the first of our three ways to make all digital products easier-to-use is simply to make them do less.

Products that do too much are potentially compromised because every feature they contain has to fit around, be compatible with, and potentially interwork with every other feature. This means that the features in the product can't **all** be designed in the best individual way to make them as useful and as usable as possible.

Products that do too much also greatly increase the risk that the user will get lost. The 80% of features most users never use get in the way of the 20% of features that they do use, 100% of the time. Too many features make it harder for users to understand what the product is about, and to find the one thing they're interested in.

Why does this happen? If it's so simple to make products easier to use by making them do less, why do we keep on making products that try to do too much? I think there are three reasons:

- Because we can. The tool that can do anything (the terrible Turing Machine) ends up doing everything, at no extra cost (except to usability).

- Because no-one knows what the product is for, or is brave enough to focus it tightly on its most valuable functions. The product becomes the union of all possible functions.

- Because sometimes people want it that way in an industry that is too often driven by number of features, instead of by the one feature everyone always wants: ease-of-use.

If you can avoid these three traps, if you can find the essence of what your product really offers your users, and if you can restrict its functions to just those most important things that everyone wants, you can immediately make your product much easier-to-use. Your users will never miss the things you didn't give them.

Even better, this same process of focussing just on the essential functions of your product can also make your own life much more straightforward when it comes to the next of our three ways to make life easier for your users — helping them understand how your product works.

Chapter 4

Mental models

It's how you **think** it works

In the previous chapter, I suggested that a good starting place for making your product easier-to-use is simply to reduce the number of features it has. Far from frustrating them, this pruning down of product functionality will make your users' lives much easier.

It turns out though that that same simplification is about to make your own life easier too. We're now going to turn to the second of our three ways to improve usability, where you'll find that the fewer features your product has, the easier it will be for you to apply the approach I'll outline here.

Although we ought to be focussing on making our users' lives easier rather than our own, this is one of those rare places where our interests are aligned. So if you think a bit more pruning of your product's features might be possible, now would be a good time to do it. Otherwise, let's move on.

Ease-of-use depends on understanding. That might sound like a platitude — so obvious as to be devoid of any useful meaning — and you might reasonably wonder why I'm even going to the trouble of saying it. After all, if users understood how the product they're trying to use actually worked, they'd find it much easier and more rewarding to use, wouldn't they? That much is obvious. Isn't it? Looking at the state of too many products in use today, I'm afraid to say I don't agree.

Most users don't understand how digital technology works, and neither do they want to. Most of us techies, if we thought about it, would agree that our users shouldn't **have** to understand how the products they use actually work. That's our job. That's what makes us "special" (in so many ways). So what can we do? How can we help our users understand and hence more easily use the products we design and deliver?

The answer, I believe, depends on what we think it means to *understand* how something works. If we can appreciate how our users think a product works (that's right, how they **think** it works), there's a better chance we can explicitly design that product to be easier-to-understand. And if we can make it easier to understand, it'll very likely become easier-to-use.

In this chapter, we're going to talk about why it might be that ordinary users can understand some things with ease, but find other things mysteriously baffling. We're going to consider how we can use that understanding to create digital products that are themselves understandable. And we're going to learn that deliberately creating that understanding is actually not hard to do, and very well worth while. Understand? Good.

Before we do all that though, we have to tackle that question of what it means to understand something. The notions we're going to address here represent significant areas of enquiry for people like psychologists, philosophers, and others who study and claim to understand how people think and reason about the world we live in. There are many competing and complementary theories and hypotheses in this area that have taken centuries to develop, and which in some cases are still the subject of development and intense debate.

I'm not about to claim any significant expertise in these often sophisticated ideas — but I don't need to be an expert in them to do a good job of designing easy-to-use products, and neither do you. In fact, I want to show you that by having a simple and almost certainly naïve understanding of some basic principles of human thinking*, you can magically make the digital products you design easier to understand for your users.

Let's begin.

---

* It even turns out not to matter too much whether these ideas about human thinking are "correct" or not. For our purposes, they work as a useful model of the world, which is actually what this chapter is all about.

Understanding depends on predictability

I'm going to start by suggesting that something is understandable (and hence, easy-to-use) if and only if it is **predictable**. It's that simple.

Again, this may sound rather obvious, and in fact it's true almost by definition. In science for example, one test of whether you "understand" a system is whether you can correctly predict the future behaviour or state of that system. If you can predict it, you can claim to understand it in some way. If you can't predict what the system is going to do under all circumstances in the future, and explain "why" it did everything it did in the past, you can't be said to fully understand it.

The same thing applies to human relationships. Someone who is predictable — a person who always responds in the same way to the same stimulus — is probably easier to understand and get along with than someone whose responses seem random or unpredictable. Of course in humans this predictably is often considered boring, and we may enjoy and find stimulation in the sometimes unexpected and unpredictable behaviour of our fellow human beings. Such is humanity. But for digital products, we don't usually find such unpredictable behaviour nearly so attractive. In fact, I think it's one of the top causes of users' frustration with digital products. The often overheard complaint, *"the system just behaves randomly"*, or the rhetorical question, *"What on earth is it doing?"*, are both pretty damning judgements of poor usability, and all too frequently heard.

Now, as techies we know that the behaviour of digital products is almost never random — it's precisely defined by the software in all but the most exceptional of circumstances. Even if that software has bugs and tells the system to do things we didn't mean or expect it to do, its behaviour is still precisely defined by the software. We just didn't write the software correctly. As techies we tend to understand how the product or system we're creating or using actually works "in reality", so its behaviour seems almost completely predictable to us. That's why a techie can pick up a product they've never used before, and can often work out how to use it. It was designed, after all, by other techies who thought in pretty much the same ways that you do. When it comes down to it, most technology works in similar ways.

Think about this though. If you're a techie helping a user to understand a new product or system, and you can make sense of it when he or she cannot, you're almost certainly using some underlying understanding of how you think it was probably implemented by the other techies who built it. You may not even realise you're doing this, but when the person you're helping says *"how did you know to do that?"*, or *"how did you know that that would fix it?"*, I'm willing to bet that if you think about it carefully you'll realise it was because you subconsciously guessed how the product was working "under the hood", and that's what gave you the edge over your ordinary user friend.

To those ordinary users, this seems like wizardry, because to people who don't understand either the details or even the principles of the underlying technology, the behaviour of all but the best digital products can seem random and unpredictable. They simply don't understand it, and as a result the product becomes or remains unusable for them. They haven't got the techie's innate understanding of the patterns of behaviour (and, importantly, common misbehaviour) of digital products, so the behaviour they see and have to interact with can seem utterly inexplicable and incomprehensible. It's this near-magical understanding of how digital things work under the covers that I said I wanted to bottle and give to users at the beginning of this book. But you'll remember I decided that that approach was the wrong way around, and that there is a better way. Read on.

Predictability depends on having a model

I'm now going to assert more formally what I've already suggested above. I'm going to assert that we humans understand the world because we have in our heads what we'll call a *model* of how the world works. This model offers us almost a parallel world that exists only in our minds. We might choose to think of it as a set of rules that define how the world appears to work. Whether it actually is such a set of rules or not doesn't matter. It's just useful for us to think of it that way. It's a bit like the relationship between the map of a landscape and the real terrain it describes. The map gives us an easy shortcut way to think about and plan our actions in the real world.

We can use this model in our heads to check, to predict, and yes — to **understand** — how the real world will behave under any conditions we might imagine or observe. We can pretend that we might do this by unconsciously running the model in our heads ahead of events in the real world. So if we're trying to make something happen, we can use the model to test and decide on a way to cause that thing to happen before we invoke the mechanism to make it happen in the real world.

We can also use these models in our head to understand what might have "caused" something that's already occurred to happen in the real world. We can run the model in reverse, after the fact, to look for conditions that would have given rise to the state we observe, and can then (if we choose) assume that those conditions indeed caused the effect.

If you want to know more about this theory of thinking using mental models of the world, start by searching online for the idea of *constructivism*. You'll find lots to read. But for our purposes here, that's more than enough theory for now. Back to the practice.

As an example, think about the personal video recorder (PVR) that many of us now have under our TVs. It has a very simple mental model. It records any programmes I chose from the programme guide, and stores them inside itself. I can play those programmes back one or more times (strictly, zero or more times, but now I sound too much like a computer scientist — or the other members of my family who record lots of things that they never get around to watching), and I can delete them (whether I've watched them or not). I can play back one programme whilst I record another (and sometimes two others). The box has a fixed capacity, and when it's full I can't record any new programmes until I delete some old ones.

It's that simple, and this clarity of mental model is perhaps one of the reasons why PVRs have been so successful at displacing our much more complex (from a user point-of-view) VCRs. But underneath, PVRs are anything but simple. Think of the software complexity that's required to deliver this experience — of all the files that have to written to, managed, and read from disk; of all the real-time requirements; and of the complex information processing that has to go on to deal with the encoded signals in the first place. The important thing though is that the user neither sees nor needs to understand **any** of this. He never needs to install new drivers or codecs (unlike on his desktop PC), he never needs to manage the file structure, and he never needs to defragment the hard disk (he doesn't even need to know that it is a hard disk in there, although most users will). None of this "reality" needs to leak into the simple, predicable and robust mental model that the PVR offers its users.

When PVRs first appeared, there were those in the techie community who said, *"Why do we need these? My PC can do all of that."* No it can't — at least not for 99% of ordinary users for whom the product is the experience it offers. The mental model is the most important part of that experience. The mental model **is** the product, and although a PC with the right hardware and software can technically do exactly what a PVR does, the mental models involved (not to say the user-experience too) are completely different. For ease-of-use, it's the mental model that matters.

I have always referred to these "models in my head" as *mental models*, which is the title of this chapter. I find that using that name helps me remember that we're talking about things that exist only in the mind. Other people sometimes use different terms to mean the same or a similar thing, including phrases like *conceptual model*, which creates a useful contrast with *implementation model* (how it really works). Another good name is *user model* which helps us remember that we're talking about the way the user (not the techie) thinks the product works. Don't worry too much about these different terms. Just remember that the model we're talking about (whatever we choose to call it) is an explanation of how someone else (not you) **thinks** the product works, and it's the basis for their understanding of how to use it. The model is how they attempt to make sense of what's happening in the real world of your product.

What we should be clear about though is that this modelling is almost always unconscious on the part of users. Sometimes we might think things through explicitly, but almost all our understanding of the world is based on the unconscious application of models. Or at least, I'm going to contend that it is, because it helps me design better digital products, which is what matters here. That's my model of the world, and I'm sticking with it. If you're a psychologist or philosopher, you might have a different view — a different model — but now we're getting ahead of ourselves.

The case of the missing model

So, people use models to understand and make sense of the world. That means that products that aren't designed to work in a way that supports a clear and straightforward mental model are almost guaranteed to be difficult to understand and use. If you find yourself thinking *"I'm not sure what this thing does or how to use it"*, that's a sure sign of what I like to refer to as a missing mental model.

You can quite often spot an even more obvious sign that a mental model is missing. For example, I took the photographs below at a railway station several years ago, and they're part of a collection I keep.

You'd think that the task of paying for a car parking ticket would be simple, but the machine shown in the photo on the left has such a confusing behaviour — it offers such a poor mental model — that the operators of the car park have had to add an after-the-fact notice (shown in the close-up on the right), that attempts to explain how to achieve the simple result of successfully buying a ticket. *"Paying by credit card? Here's how.", it says.* But buying a ticket is the only thing this machine lets you do, and many people will want to pay by credit card. And yet this machine manages to make it confusing, not actively, but by omission. It simply doesn't offer a clear mental model of what's going on.

Whenever you see a notice like this (often hand-written and stuck on a machine by exasperated staff), or find yourself compelled to buy one of those carefully written and beautifully explained third-party manuals for a software product you can't understand, just remember — it's not the manual that's missing, it's the mental model!

What these kind people are doing — these people who put up notices, or write "how to" books (including this one), or sit and patiently explain to others how something works — what they're doing is giving you a way to think about the product or system. They're giving you a mental model. I know this, because I frequently do it myself when I help other people use a product I've had to work hard to understand. The giveaways are phrases like *"it works like this"*, *"I think about it this way"*, or as in the photo above, *"here's how"*.

Once again, if you find yourself explaining to someone else how best they should think about how a product works (whether it was designed by you or by someone else), that's a mental model being transferred from your brain to theirs. At that moment, you can ask yourself, *"is this a good model, or is there a better one?"*

There's more than one way to model a cat

Having suggested that people reason about the world using what we're calling mental models, we can now consider properly what I hinted at earlier: that different people might have different mental models of the same real world thing.

Remember that the model is the map, not the terrain, so it's fine for there to be multiple models that describe the world in potentially completely different ways. They might describe it at different levels of detail for example, or they might rely on different knowledge, or be based on differing assumptions. They might even seek to explain only a subset of the behaviour, or to explain it only approximately.

We see this effect in science too. Explanations of how the world behaves (scientific hypotheses, theories, and laws) have regularly had to be revised or improved as it became clear that they didn't predict the world as accurately as it could be measured.

Designing and flying communication satellites, for example, means that you have to understand Einstein's theories. If you don't, your satellites don't work. But to predict when a falling brick will hit the ground you only need to remember Newton's much simpler laws that we all learnt at school (you do remember Newton's laws, don't you?). In fact, of course, even if you don't remember Newton's laws, your experience in the real world gives you a good enough understanding of how physical things behave that's usually perfectly good enough to live life quite happily, just as people always did before Newton and Einstein came along. This "folk" or "pop" understanding of how things work is one inspiration we can use when we look shortly at how to explicitly design a good mental model.

The important point here is that the model is not the real thing. Instead it's an abstract thing that can be used to explain, to predict, and to understand the behaviour of the real thing, but it is not how it "really" works. This means that it can be both simpler and potentially **completely different** from the real thing, and in fact (as we shall shortly see) almost all good mental models are both of those things.

Inferring the mental model

As human beings, we always try to make sense of the world by building these mental models (at least, that's what constructivism says). If you're conscious of this, you can observe yourself trying to infer the rules of engagement (the mental model) next time you're struggling with a particularly recalcitrant piece of new technology. It won't be long. You'll hear yourself thinking, *"What's the logic here? How is this thing organised? How does it* **work***?"*. That'll be you trying to infer a mental model from the behaviour of the product.

Children — babies in particular — usually do this very naturally and easily as part of growing up. They simply observe what goes on around them — sometimes literally as passive observers, and sometimes as active participants — and start to build in their heads an understanding that makes the world seem predictable and understandable. Having such a model in their heads makes the world feel like a safer place and a more pleasurable thing to interact with.

Isn't that what we want for our digital products too?

The ease with which children build these models may well be one of the reasons that they appear to have such an enhanced facility with technology, compared to older people whose models of the world are perhaps more "complete" and less easily changed or built upon. Children observe the behaviour of the product, and somehow manage to infer a model that delivers to them an understanding that baffles and impresses older users in equal measure.

This creation of a model by children applies even to the simplest things, like conservation of mass — the idea that if you cut a cake in two you may well have two pieces of cake, but each will be half the size of the original. The world is full of these simple, universal, and invariant (never-changing) rules.

Sometimes this so-called *inductive* learning (where you work out the rules from examples) is augmented by being explicitly told — or taught — what the rules are. But one way or another, a model usually gets created in people's minds, and those few individuals who cannot do this are unfortunately destined to find the aspects of life for which they cannot build a reliable model very challenging indeed. Just like the users of most digital products in fact, for which it is often almost impossible (for adults, at least) to intuit a useful and predictive mental model.

Just as babies do in the real world, so your users will try hard to build a mental model of your product. They will look at it, prod it and poke it, observe how it responds, and try to understand "how it works", usually as part of using or playing with it. In that sense, they're just like babies trying to work out how the world behaves. Just like babies, except that users usually have neither the time, nor the patience, to spend several years learning your product. In fact, with more and more products and services, users may only use them once (like the ticket machine above) and have only a few seconds to try to work out what's going on. Unfortunately, if your product is like many, it won't actually have the regular, reliable and consistent behaviour that's needed to let users quickly form a good, simple, stable model.

Very occasionally, users will read a manual – or even more occasionally they'll go on a training course. If they do that, you get your chance to tell them how your product works. You get to explicitly teach them a mental model. Increasingly though, direct interaction with your product is the only way users come to "understand" how it works, and for many products (ticket machines, many websites, and other one-off interactions for example), it's the only way they should need to use to understand your product.

This direct interaction allows users to build a model of how your product behaves, and sometimes to believe that they understand it. Unfortunately, the mental models that users build for themselves are sometimes very poor, being based on a limited range of circumstances, handicapped by the inconsistent behaviour of the product, and distorted by all sorts of sometimes strange pre-conceptions about how the product might or ought to work.

So the typical user often ends up with a very poor mental model of what should be an entirely predictable system (your product, which is made of software, and hence entirely predictable, at least by you). In fact, the user's model is sometimes so poor, that it completely fails to correctly predict the behaviour of your product. When that happens, the user is left floundering around randomly looking for or trying things. And whose fault is that? The user's for building a poor mental model of your product? Not in his mind. It's your product's fault for being — yes — unpredictable and difficult to understand.

Design the mental model first

Having argued that it's the mental model of a product that governs how easy users find that product to use, we now arrive at two almost inevitable conclusions — one obvious, the other less so.

The obvious first conclusion is that you, the product designer, should explicitly create the user's mental model for your product. You should **design** the mental model. Even if you don't do this personally, someone you're working with should. In other words, someone responsible for what the product does should carefully decide what the right mental model for the users of your product is. Some people talk about one aspect of creating a new product in terms of *designing the user-experience*, and the creation of a suitable mental model is a vital part of this process.

What you should **not** do is to leave this process to

chance, hoping that the user can create for himself some sort of simplified version of the way you understand the product as its technical creator. The mental model does not have to reflect how the software underneath actually works at all. In fact, it should almost never do that. Instead it should offer a conceptually simpler understanding of what the product does and how it behaves in terms that make sense to the user (whoever he may be) in his domain.

Once again, you should not leave this process of creating a mental model to chance. Instead, you should explicitly design a mental model — a map or master plan — of the product for your user. We'll talk shortly about what makes a good model, and how to design one, keeping in mind the rule above that this model is not the same as your understanding of how the product actually works. The important point is to make the creation of this user's view of how your product works and what it does an explicit design act, and not an act of chance to be undertaken afresh by each new user every time they encounter your product for the first time.

When I introduced the idea of a mental model above, I talked about its creation as a way to explain, understand, and predict the behaviour of a product. I talked about it as if the product came first, and the mental model was created in the user's mind to explain the behaviour of the product afterwards. And that's the way it often is. But I'm now going to suggest that it should actually be the other way around. Our second conclusion is therefore that the mental model should be designed **first**, and that the product should implement and deliver the mental model, rather than be explained by it after the fact. I'll say it again. You should design the mental model first — **before** you design the software or the product that will implement it.

In this respect, the mental model **is** the product, and the digital technology exists merely to create and maintain the illusion that the model is actually really the way the product works. I say "merely" with the greatest respect, of course, without forgetting the amount of effort needed to implement good software. I was a working software engineer for long enough to know that pulling off the acts of magic required to deliver the illusion of a good mental model is a major feat, sometimes **the** major feat of a good product (more on that in the next chapter on aesthetics).

Don Norman, a highly respected expert and writer on product design, has described this idea as *"writing the user manual first"*. The notion is that if you write the manual first, you'll be able to describe how you'd like the product to behave, how it ought to behave, and not have to resort to trying to make sense post-hoc of how the product actually [mis-]behaves. I've found that idea inspiring for many years, but since so few people actually read the user manual, and since I'm arguing that ideally it shouldn't even be necessary to have or to read a manual, I now prefer to think of this same idea as *"designing the mental model first"*.

I simply can't overstate the importance of this idea of explicitly designing the mental model for the product — and doing it first. Too many products are conceived as technical edifices onto which a "user interface" is layered to provide some sort of translation between how the product actually works, and the poor user who must use it. But for so many products today, the *user-experience* is the product. What the product does for the user is what they buy, not how it does it.

Do not, therefore, think of putting a user-interface **onto** your product. Think instead of explicitly designing the user experience (the mental model) — without reference to the software that will implement it* — and then build the software to deliver that experience. In these terms, your product then **is** the experience it offers to your users, however differently it might actually work underneath.

What makes a good mental model?

If you've followed the story so far, we now come to the question that should by now be bursting from your lips: *"How do I design a good mental model for my product?"*. Let's talk about that.

I'm afraid I don't have a simple answer for you. I can't offer you a straightforward process, recipe or algorithm that will always produce a good result. Coming up with, designing, and fleshing out a good mental model is, I'm afraid to say, a creative act, and it needs to be tackled in whatever ways work for you and the team you work in.

---

* I know. In reality this has to be an iterative experience, like the interplay between great architecture and building technology. But the important point is that the user experience should drive the software design, and not the other way around!

Like all creative acts though, you will usually find that your first idea is not your best, so it pays to generate lots of ideas. It also pays to look outside your own context for existing ideas, and for stimulation for new ones. There are lots of books on innovation, so if you find coming up with new ideas hard, you might like to try any of the many techniques that have been offered by others.

Although I can't help you to have good ideas (at least, not here, but feel free to ask me afterwards), what I can help you to do is to evaluate and judge the ideas you come up with. I can offer you some heuristics that help you to predict whether any given candidate mental model you come up with might turn out to be a good one in real life.

Ultimately, you will want to (and you must) test your ideas with real users, and again there are many books that cover ways and processes for doing just that. But before you get to user-testing, you'll need to whittle down your ideas to just those you can afford to prototype and test (in whatever form). To do that it helps if you can predict which ideas might work well in practice, and which are doomed before you begin. That way you can focus on the things that are most likely to work. That's what I try to do, and this is how I usually do it.

Simplicity

The first thing I look for is **simplicity**. There's that word again, and if you're not sure what I mean when I use it, you might like to go back and re-read the previous chapter.

What's a mental model again? It's a set of simple and invariant rules of behaviour. A model should be as simple as possible (but no simpler — see below). The fewer "rules" that are required, the fewer concepts that are involved, the fewer exceptions to the rules, the better and easier it will be for your users to understand what's going on. That should be your goal.

However, if you're clever and you think very hard, it's sometimes possible to reduce a mental model to startling simplicity — or at least to a startling smallness. When this happens, it's usually achieved by creating some very abstract notions that stand in for the concrete concepts we deal with in everyday life. Computer scientists in particular (and mathematicians, philosophers, and other thinkers in general) are particularly prone to this kind of reductionism. It is very appealing to them because it's a powerful tool of their trade, but ordinary users can easily get left behind.

Be careful that the mental model you create isn't too clever, and that it deals with concepts only at the level of abstraction users are used to. It's no co-incidence, for example, that iTunes talks about *songs*, and not about *sound files* (a more general notion), or *media assets* (more general still). It's songs that users love and want to buy, not files.

Regularity

The next thing I think is highly desirable in any mental model is **regularity**. Does everything work in the same way? Can I perform every operation on every object, at least where it makes sense? Can I re-use what I've learnt in one part of the product to help me predict and hence understand how another part of the product behaves? Or conversely, does one part of the product behave in an arbitrarily different way from another.

It's sometimes observed that we build products whose structure reflects the structure of the team that built them. In these circumstances, each part of the product may behave in equally usable, but unnecessarily different ways. If you look for this effect you can spot that it is rife in some quite major and successful products, particularly after a few years of development. Don't let it happen to you. Don't let the structure of your team define the behaviour of your product. Instead, keeping going through your product — combing it if you like — to try to get everything lined up, parallel and regular. I have a little obsession with tidiness and consistency, which would probably make me a terrible interior or landscape designer. But I think it really helps to adopt that obsessive persona when it comes to designing easy-to-use products, where the more you can make things work the same way, the better. Novelty is not your goal. Neither are surprise or intrigue (unless you're designing a game).

Pre-existing models

Another question to ask yourself when creating the mental model is, *"who is this product for?"*. What do they already understand, and how do they already think about the world?

What concepts already exist in this user's space that you can re-use in your product?

A good example is the *basket* or *cart* that is now universal on e-shopping websites. It's a straightforward model that users easily understand because of their prior experience of the physical world.

A good model does **not** have to be metaphorical though. Do not – I repeat, **do not** – force your model into being a metaphorical representation of the real world if it doesn't suit it. Yes, shopping baskets, trash cans and desktops have all worked well in their place, but users are capable of reasoning about imaginary things too, like hyperlinks and playlists.

However, I do think you should respect some of the rules of the physical world. For example, conservation laws are important. Things shouldn't come and go or change by themselves, and you should take great care if things are going to appear in more than one place at the same time.

That last point is a classic trap. As software folks we're very used to the idea of seeing objects (the same objects) through more than one view or filter. But non-technical users can struggle with this idea if they're not used to it. Be careful with things like files that appear in more than one folder because they happen to match whatever filter is being applied. It can be terribly confusing, because it doesn't happen in the real world whose metaphor is being claimed by the model. Sometimes it can be better to restrict the set of ways of getting at something if that helps to make the mental model more robust. You should be prepared to make these sorts of trade-off.

My favourite example of a model that's broken because it doesn't respect the way users think comes from my local supermarket. There they have a set of self-scan checkouts where customers can scan and pack shopping themselves, and then pay the machine. But not everything has a barcode. So when I come across one of those barcode-less items in my basket, I have to tell the machine what it is (a red pepper, or bag of tomatoes, and so on). But **before** I can do that, I have to tell the machine whether it is *"fruit and vegetables"* (that is, sold by weight) or *"non-weigh produce"* (that is, sold by number). Only then can I choose the item from a menu. But if I'm buying red peppers, for example, I don't know which it is. Are they sold by weight or quantity? I have to guess, and if I get it wrong I have to search up and down a long list before I decide it might not be there. What I should be able to do is simply to tell the machine I'm buying red peppers and have it direct me either to weigh the bag or tell it how many I've got as appropriate. I'm willing to bet that this model of the world reflects how the supermarket thinks about its stock *behind the scenes* as being divided into these two categories. It certainly doesn't represent my (the customer's) natural view of the world.

Representation and discovery

Good models are also amenable to straightforward and clear **representation**. We'll talk most about this in the next chapter, but if you've created a model that is hard to represent through whatever technology your user interacts with (whether for design or technical reasons), think again about whether it's the right model. Like many of the suggestions I'm offering, there may well be a bit of to-ing and fro-ing involved here, a bit of iteration and creative tension, before you get the balance right.

Then, if a model is capable of straightforward representation, there's a good chance that it and the features your product embodies, will also be **discoverable**. Remember that our goal here is (or should be) to create a product that does not require the user to read a manual (either first or later) in order to find out all the great things the product can do (hopefully not too many things though).

Direct manipulation

Another useful test for a good model is whether it is capable of being **directly manipulated**. It's always better if the user can control your system by directly interacting with whatever representation of the model you've implemented (by touching or dragging an object or whatever), than if he is forced to indirectly manipulate the same object by typing, interacting with a dialogue or menu, or setting numerical preferences, for example.

This sort of interaction is becoming more and more common, although sometimes it's possible to confuse users by offering a function via a direct manipulation that the user doesn't even realise is there and so can't find, so it pays to be a little bit careful about that.

Unfortunately, implementing direct manipulation is

almost always more work than other approaches, but at the risk of anticipating the case I'll make in the next chapter, it's work you have to invest only once, whereas every one of your users benefits from your investment every time he uses your product. The cost of implementation is a one-off; the benefits are long-lasting.

Sense of control

In almost all systems, the user should be **in control** (or at least offered the illusion that that's the case). What I say goes (I mean "I" as a user of your product, not "I" as the writer of this book). I cannot, for example, understand why a whole series of DVD players that I've owned seem to have better things to do than to immediately open the drawer when I press the eject button, rather than opening it after 10-15 seconds of doing I have no idea what. What could possibly be more important than opening the drawer when I ask it to (other than stopping the disk, which does **not** take that long)?

Feedback

The previous point introduces the next test for a good model — that it should be capable of naturally offering the user good **feedback** as to the state of the system. Ideally, this feedback and the **direct manipulation** that provides **control** should all be combined into the same thing.

The real world is good at this. The position of a knob tells me what value is set, and I can change that value by altering the position of the knob. Simple. As I've suggested though, you don't have to create a metaphorical model (in fact, you should be healthily wary of doing so), but the physical world still sets a good standard when it comes to interaction and feedback.

No hidden states

In a similar vein, there should not be any **hidden states** in your model — things that change the behaviour of the system but which the user cannot see (at least, not easily).

The existence of such hidden states is of course what's behind the old and by now infamous advice from IT departments everywhere to *"try turning it off and on again"*, or *"uninstall and re-install the software"*, since both these actions tend to reset hidden states back to their clean condition. (I myself have a rule with my family – do not ask me to help make your gadget work unless you've tried rebooting it first.)

If you try not to put any of these hidden states into your model, we can hope that your users will eventually learn to stop performing these little bits of voodoo in their attempts to reset their products into a working state, and everyone's lives will get a bit easier.

Task orientation

Another thing to remember is that users are often oriented towards some **task** that they're trying to accomplish, and that that task isn't usually "interacting with your product" (unless they're a nerd, a gamer, or a product test engineer). Understanding what these tasks or goals are can help you create a suitable mental model.

My favourite example of a failure here is our family's bread-maker machine, which offers a delay feature so that we can wake up in the morning to the smell of freshly baked bread. Wonderful. The only problem is that it does this by requiring me to tell it how far in the future from now I want the bread to be ready. So at 21:35 I have to work out in my head how many hours and minutes it is until 07:45. Quick! Answer as soon as you buzz. Every night. Why can't I simply tell the machine that I want the bread to be ready at 07:45? That's the goal I'm trying to achieve. Of course, this would require the device to have an internal clock, and this bread-maker seems to be one of the very few electronic devices I own where the manufacturer has decided not to include one. But it would be so much easier if the designers of this product had realised that I want bread at a **particular time of day**, and not **after a particular delay**, and designed this interaction to support that.

Whilst we're on the subject though, unless your product **is** a clock, or **needs** a clock, please don't put a clock in it just because you can. How many clocks do you think the average person needs to keep setting and re-setting at least twice a year? (If your clock can be set automatically — and provided it is only set that way — you are possibly excused from following this rule.)

Product as a medium

In a related vein, a user's task-orientation means that he will generally be thinking of doing things **with** or **through** your product, not **to** it. If you can regard your product as *mediating* those interactions, whether they are with some content or information to which your product allows access, or with other people or entities to which your product connects your user, you will often end up with a better mental model.

Remember that there are almost always three parties involved in the interactions you're designing: your user; your product; and the thing your user is using your product as a tool to act upon. Of these three things, the first and last are the most important. If you can make the second thing (your product) as invisible as possible, so much the better. Sorry.

No implementation leakage

Finally, check your model thoroughly for any characteristics that are leaking through from the proposed **implementation**. Is there anything that works the way it does from the point-of-view of the user mainly or entirely because it works that way from the point-of-view of the techie building the system? If there is, think hard about whether it needs to be that way, and change it if it does not.

A classic example here is the *File>Save* model that almost all desktop PC software has had for decades. It comes from the underlying fact that the machine does its work in RAM (which is small and volatile), so that things you want to store permanently have to be moved to and from disk (which is large and persistent). But why does the user have to know this is happening, and even more so, why does he have to control it? When it comes to virtual memory, for example, the underlying technology happily manages the RAM and the disk interchangeably, so why not for documents? This old model is just beginning to be broken these days, although it has become so ingrained in users' mental models of how computers work that it's now quite hard to reverse.

Summary

The second of our three ways to make digital products easier to use is really the meat in the sandwich of this book. In the previous chapter, I set the scene by talking about stripping your product down to just its core features. In the next chapter we'll top things off by talking about the visual (or other sensory) implementation of your design. But here, in this chapter, I've argued that if your users are to understand the concept, purpose and functioning of your product, they must have a good mental framework on which to hang that understanding. We've called that framework a **mental model**, and over the previous few pages I've tried to convince you of a number of things about that model:

- That it doesn't have to be the same as your understanding of how the product actually works. In fact, it almost never is the same. The user is not you.

- That the mental model is not something that serendipitously comes into being the first time a user uses your product. Neither does it emerge as you design the implementation. Instead, you should **explicitly** design the mental model as part of the user-experience of using your product.

- That you should not only explicitly design the mental model, but that you should do it **first**, before you think (too hard) about how your product will be implemented. Then you should make the software implement that model. Perfectly.

- That you should seek to make the make the mental model **inferable** from the user's experience of using your product. Make it so they can work it out just by seeing it and using it. That way, your product won't need a user manual at all.

If you can do these things, and especially if you can do the last, you'll create a product that your users will find easy-to-use, but they won't know why. That's magic, of the very best sort. And well worth struggling hard for.

And that's the hard part over. We're on the home straight now, as we move on to look at the last of the three ways we might make all digital products better. It's time to talk about how things look.

Chapter 5

Aesthetics

The benefits of beauty

We now come to the third and final of my suggestions for how every digital product might be made better. And it is perhaps the most controversial, at least among software engineers.

I've already talked about how you can make your product easier-to-use by reducing the number of things it does (making it *simple*), and by introducing a strong *mental model*. I'm now about to argue that it also really matters how your product *looks* (or how it *feels*, how it *sounds*, or perhaps even how it *smells* — if that's appropriate for your product).

Executed well, good aesthetics supports the other two ways that I've suggested digital products might be improved. It sets the scene for, reinforces and delivers on the promises made by the other two — simplicity and mental models. It is, I believe, properly regarded as an equal partner in our inter-linked trio of techniques.

I'm not, I'm afraid, going to offer much help here on **how** you might make your product more aesthetically pleasing, or even what aesthetic pleasure actually **is**. That's up to you, and it depends on the sensibilities of your own market and customers, your own skills and those of others you can access or employ. Instead, I'm going to advance a number of arguments as to **why** you and everyone involved in creating your product should care passionately about aesthetics, and **why** you should invest a worthwhile proportion of your efforts to make your product easy-to-use on making your product also a pleasure-to-use. Actually deciding to do this is usually the hardest part. Any number of people and organisations can help you to do it once you decide you want to do it.

For the same reason, I'm not going to offer you too many examples in this chapter. I don't think you need them to understand the arguments I'm going to make, and I want to focus on the **value** of investing in aesthetics, rather than on the **process** of doing so.

I'm also going to assume that we're talking here about interactions between humans and machines that are largely visual. That is, we're dealing with dialogues that take place through a screen or something similar. However, the same arguments really do apply to interactions that happen mechanically (through physical buttons, for example), aurally (on the phone, for example), or via our other senses.

Now, there are those in the techie community who think that aesthetics is somehow *effete*. They think it of it as expensive, pointless, trivial, lacking in vigour, feckless, marked by self-indulgence, decadent, wasteful of engineering resources, pretentious, elitist, and just not the sort of thing that proper engineers should be involved with. Otherwise it's just fine, of course.

I disagree. I believe — as I've said above — that aesthetics should be of first-class concern in the design of easy-to-use products. But I don't want to offer just my opinion or preference for things that are "beautiful" over things that are "ugly". I want to suggest a slew of concrete reasons as to why I think it's worth making a significant investment to make your product **pleasurable** as well as **functional,** and I want to explain how I think that paying attention to aesthetics can directly and powerfully influence ease-of-use (which is why we're here, of course). I want to persuade you that aesthetics is a first-class factor that you should be paying attention to if you care at all about ease-of-use.

Don't think you can escape if you're not building a consumer product either. Just because your users are gnarly-handed tradespeople who take things as they find them, or highly-paid professionals who have higher things to worry about than how something looks, doesn't mean that aesthetics doesn't matter. We're all human, and we all respond in similar ways, no matter how rough-and-ready or highbrow the context might be.

I chose the title of this chapter with some care. The word *aesthetics* refers to the ways in which our senses and emotions react to a given stimulus (at least it does when I use it). That's what I'm going to talk about here. I also used another word above — *sensibility* — whose origins are in the Latin term for *"that which can be perceived by the senses"*. In this chapter, that's what matters, as I'm about to explain. Let's consider the various ways that good aesthetics actually help deliver good usability.

Setting the scene

Our first experience of nearly any product is almost certainly that of how it impinges on our senses. This *first impression*, like all first impressions, counts. Whether we like it or not, it immediately results in our forming an opinion about the product we're going to interact with. We form a nascent point-of-view about whether it's going to be a pleasure or a pain, whether it's going to be easy or hard, even whether we want to bother trying to use it at all.

If it's a positive reaction, we might call this effect, as product designers do, *delight*. There are lots of things we might call it if it's negative, but my favourite is perhaps the word *dread*. I think this best describes the feeling you get when you know you're going to have to do battle with a poorly-designed product. The question is, do you want your product to be *delight*ful or *dread*ful?

Psychologists use an unusual version of an apparently familiar word to describe our emotional state at any given time. They refer to our emotional response to stimuli using the noun, *affect* (with the emphasis on the first syllable – AFFect). From there we get the everyday term, *affection*, and the technical term *affective computing* — a special type of computing that deliberately sets out to influence or respond to human emotions. But I would argue that **all** interactions with computing influence our emotions, and as the personal frustration I expressed in earlier chapters reveals, not always positively.

So if influencing your users' emotions is unavoidable, shouldn't you be trying to do it positively? Just as your own personal appearance influences your likely success at a job interview (even though you might argue or wish that it shouldn't), so the appearance of your product influences your users' likely success at using it.

One concrete reason I'm going to suggest this might be so is that a positive *affect* (there's that word again) may well make your user temporarily more tolerant, more engaged, and more willing to spend the few moments of time it takes to figure out even the best of interaction designs. It gets your user on your side whilst you convince him (through your product design) that it's worth understanding how to make use of the product. It starts the dialogue between your user and your product on the right foot.

Of course, a positive affect has all sorts of other benefits beyond ease-of-use, such as increasing the likelihood that people will **buy** your product, and increasing the amount of money they might **pay** for it. Organisations may buy with their heads, but people (including people inside organisations) buy with their hearts.

If people feel delighted by the experience of using your product, they are also more likely to talk about it with others, and more likely to tell those others how easy it was to use. In that way, the positive feelings even of people who have yet to actually use your product are set up prior to their first experience of your product in the flesh. Soon, a myth of ease-of-use grows around your product, and hordes of delighted users will happily forgive even the most glaring errors you might still make in the simplicity or elegant mental model you're trying to deliver.

Much as you may hate wearing a suit for an interview, putting your product into a smart set of clothes can make a big difference to the way it's received. It's even true that a certain element of non-functional delight can be valuable here too. Product designers sometimes deliberately introduce small features (*delighters*) specifically to provoke a positive emotional response. There was a time in the 1980's when damped soft-eject cassette decks fulfilled this function. Today, a similar momentary smile is provoked by the way the little orange aeroplane icon actually **flies** onto the corner of the screen instead of just appearing when I select airplane-mode on my phone. It probably only took someone an hour or so to program that, but it's worth it a thousand times or more every day.

What you must **not** do though, is hire a designer and allow him or her to create a visual appearance that prioritises a particular kind of aesthetics **above** usability. Hiding things away (so they appear only when you touch them, for example), reducing font sizes too much, putting dark grey text on a slightly darker grey background, all sorts of things like this might be considered "artistic", "elegant", even (heaven forbid) "avant garde", but they kill usability. You should not (unless, perhaps, you are designing a game), be attempting to create a sense of mystery or intrigue around how to interact with your product. Your user-interface is not a work of art. You are simply attempting to create a positive affect through good design. That's all.

Simplicity is beautiful

Having got past first impressions, let me now explain how and why I think aesthetics truly supports the other two principles I've offered, starting with *simplicity*.

Simplicity, I hope you recall, is all about doing less. It's about removing functions that aren't really needed, because of the clutter they create in the user's understanding of what the product really does, and because of how they make it harder to design a good and effective way for the user to navigate the product's important functions.

Aesthetics has an important part to play here too. For example, the removal of visual clutter (or its equivalent in other senses) allows the user to see the "meat" of the interaction. This is a not dissimilar idea to the notion of **chart junk** coined by Edward Tufte in his celebrated book *The Visual Display of Information*. Tufte recommends that we remove excess visual devices from graphs and other representations (noisy grid lines, unnecessary colours, meaningless visual decoration) so as to allow the **information** to shine through. I like to see the same thing done to digital products to allow the **functionality** to shine through.

In this context, visual clutter also means the implicit visual clutter caused when actual visual elements fail to line up as they should, or when they are unnecessarily different in design. These random variations in layout are implicit clutter that can be just as distracting to the user, and just as damaging to the impression of simplicity we should be trying to convey. To avoid this effect, it's well worth learning even a little bit about typography and graphic design, both of whose positive effects stem from a **reduction** in variance and the introduction of more or less rigorously applied patterns (known as grids, but not usually visible as such) through which visual elements are laid out with a sense of order and relevance.

Once again, my aim here is not to tell you **how** to do this, but simply to suggest that it is an important and valuable use of your resources to do so. Worrying about whether things line up visually may sometimes seem like the equivalent of *fiddling while Rome burns*, or *re-arranging deckchairs on the Titanic* if the core functionality of the product isn't working. Of course, whether your product works and is bug free (!) is job number one, but it doesn't cost much to make things look neat and tidy too, and it brings some serious benefits.

The visual design of an interaction is also very revealing of its true simplicity. It's hard to make an unnecessarily complex interaction (by which I mean one with too many ifs, buts, and choices) look truly visually simple (although there are those who attempt to apply a thick veneer of false simplicity to a complex interaction in the hope of achieving the desired effect).

Whilst we as humans do, on occasion, find complexity visually appealing (for example, in the splendour of buildings designed in the gothic or baroque styles), there is no doubting the strong appeal of simplicity to our senses (for example, in Picasso's owl, camel, and similar drawings). In that regard, an interface that looks good will often look good precisely because it is simple, and being simple is (as we know now), good.

And finally, there is an affective element here again too. An immediately and obviously simple visual design (or aural design, etc) immediately conveys to the user the message that *this is going to be simple*. It says to them, *this won't hurt a bit*. It primes them to expect and look for a simple interaction experience, and invites their patience if it turns out (as is entirely possible) to be less than truly perfect.

You might argue that, wrongly applied, a simple visual design on top of a complex product sets people up for disappointment, but that's what I meant above by a *visual veneer*, and if you've been reading this book in sequence, you should know by now how and where to fix the real problem in that case (hint: it's not in the visual design).

Supporting the illusion

So, good aesthetic design communicates, supports, and reinforces simplicity. The other principle that good aesthetic design can support is the idea of the *mental model*. I hope you remember that the mental model is how the user **thinks** your product works (the model he has of it in his head), rather than the **real** way that you as its creator know that it actually works.

If you've designed a great mental model, then the job of the visual interface is to communicate and sustain that illusion (because that's what it is), without ever letting the user accidently peek under the product's skirts to experience whatever true horrors of how it really works might be lurking therein.

In this way, the visual design reveals and represents the imaginary machine that the software underneath is creating and delivering, and with which the user is supposed to interact. The more precisely and consistently it does this, the easier the user will find it to "get" the model in the first place, and the harder it will be for the illusion to be shattered accidently.

Much as a stage magician might use a host of subtle cues and tricks to collectively convey a strong impression of something that's not real or not really happening, so the interface to a digital product has to conjure up out of nothing the impression of the imaginary mental model that we hope by now the product designer has explicitly created. What this means is that **details matter**, and this is another reason why I believe that the significant effort I'm suggesting you put into the aesthetics of an interface is not the effete pursuit that I earlier accused some of believing, but a genuinely important element in delivering the proper and desirable user-experience.

For example, in a visual interface, animation is often both very expensive to deliver but also hugely helpful in conveying the mental model of the interaction. Animation means that when some object in the interface changes into something else, or when the same object moves from one context to another, the user can more easily keep track of what is happening than if such changes are simply presented as sudden discrete transitions. In this way, an animated effect that might otherwise seem like merely a "whizzy" piece of "eye-candy" (two derogatory terms sometimes applied to pointless visual showboating) is actually an important functional part of delivering an easy-to-use experience for your user. For example, scrolling through a list of items is easier for a user to understand and keep track of than paging through it — you know that from your own experience. Smooth scrolling is better (and more expensive) still.

It's important to understand that I am **not** suggesting that enormous resources should be expended to somehow recreate a visual impression **of the real world**. Remember that I said that good mental models do not have to be metaphorical. It's even less likely that a good visual design will be a precisely rendered impression of anything from the real world. For an example of what I mean by this, try searching online for images of the ill-fated *Magic Cap* user-interface. It seemed like a beautiful idea at the time, but it didn't work.

What I am saying is that as far as possible (or, of course, as far as practical, affordable, and so on) things should look and appear to behave like the abstractions they purport to be. Thus, if a menu can be "pulled down", it should look as if it is being pulled down. If something can be "opened", and if it has other things "inside" it, those illusions should be created visually. If the mental model requires the user to believe that something is "on top" of something else, it should look like that. The more care you take to make these illusions look and feel right, the less the user will notice that they are actually **illusions,** and the more invisible your interface will become. Your users will think (unconsciously, I would suggest) that that's how your product "really" works, which was the point of the mental model in the first place. You get the idea.

Feedback is also important. When something happens, the user should see the effect of that change, and the aftereffect. The little puff of smoke produced when an icon is deleted from the Apple OS X dock is undeniably cute (perhaps even too cute), but it also serves a purpose in communicating to the user what just occurred.

I happen to believe that sound effects can be important and valuable in this regard too. Not everyone agrees though. Noises coming from a digital device can be incredibly annoying in a way that real world noises are not, so users need to be provided with a way to turn them down or completely off. But done properly (and by properly, I mean in the way a foley artist produces almost inaudible but vital sound effects for mundane actions in films and TV programmes), they can add an extra layer of realism and **understanding** to an interaction. *Understanding* is the key word here, which is why I also believe that such sound effects should not be a matter of individual user choice (resulting in a potential cacophony of meaningless beeps, jingles and warbles), but a part of the conscious and consistent aesthetic design of the interaction created by its designer.

Whilst we're on the subject of user-choice, I'm also a sceptic when it comes to the value or appropriateness of letting the user personalise the aesthetics of his or her interaction with a product. It's not that I don't want to give people what they want, because there are undoubtedly good reasons why a user might want to configure things for the purpose of accessibility, or so that he can know that it's his phone ringing and not mine, or simply to arrange things the way he would like. Rather, I believe that what users want above most else is ease-of-use. To the extent that ease-of-use is supported by good aesthetic design, those aesthetics need to be considered as part of the whole design, and not as a piecemeal matter of preference for different colours, icons, backgrounds or sounds by the user. Of course though, as I suggested earlier, when the designer of a product fails to do his job in reducing the number of functions a product has, I'm only too glad to have customisation mechanisms available to let me finish it for him!

The mental model is a delicate thing. I suggested earlier that inconsistencies or incompleteness in the model can severely compromise its believability. With that in mind, I want to leave you with the impression that the visual representation of a mental model is like its reflection in a still pool of water. If, when the user reaches out to touch that model, it ripples and wobbles, it gives away the fact that it is **only** an illusion, and that illusion is effectively shattered.

If you've spent time reducing the functionality of your product — making it do less — now is the time to spend all that computing power you've freed up maintaining the illusion of whatever the user is interacting with. I advised you earlier not to worry about the computer getting bored at having so little to do if you removed lots of functions from your product. Now is the time to give it plenty to keep it occupied again. Remember that the time you invest in doing this only has to be spent once, but I believe every single user will thank you for it every single time they use your product. And you want that to be a lot.

Looks right, works right

A further reason to care about aesthetics is that it offers quite an interesting test of your interaction design. As computer scientist David Gelernter has pointed out in his book *Machine Beauty*, if something works well, there is a sense of beauty to it. A car that is aerodynamically streamlined looks appealing, and a building that looks right is often stable. This *looks right/works right* idea can be powerfully applied to the design of digital products.

For example, when I'm designing something I frequently look for and try to offer the user what I call *symmetry*. What I mean is that I'm looking for a certain regularity or orthogonality, so that if function A works on object B, then it should work the same way on object C if that's appropriate too. The system is then symmetrical.

In art, symmetry is often a disaster. As a techie, I can only bring myself to hang pictures in the middle of a wall, even though I know they look better off to one side. And it's taken me ages to understand that an odd number of plants in a flower-bed or potatoes on a plate look more pleasing than a symmetrical even number.

But in the functionality of a product, symmetry is quite often an indicator of good usability. In that regard, this type of symmetry (not necessarily visual symmetry of course, but functional symmetry) is both desirable and pleasing in an interaction design. To me, this kind of symmetry makes a product more beautiful. To a user, it makes it more usable.

I want to encourage you to make more use of your own sense of aesthetics in this way to judge what might make for pleasing user interactions with your product. And don't tell me you don't have one (a sense of aesthetics, that is). Even the most techie individuals (in fact, especially the most techie individuals) can tell when a piece of code, or a software architecture, or any sort of technical design is clean, elegant, and beautiful. Use those same skills here — remembering of course that you're applying that reasoning to the **user's** mental model of the system, and not to **your** implementation model. Don't let the two get confused — that would be a big mistake!

There's an easy test for when you've got this right. As a creator of new things, you'll be familiar with the feeling you get when you use a great product and find yourself thinking, *"I wish I'd invented that"*. You already know when something is right on the inside, and the feeling that it creates to be able to say, *"I invented that"*. Your goal here is simply to provoke that same feeling in respect of what's on the outside. I'm not suggesting it's easy, just that it's worth the effort — even personally — to try to achieve it.

And that brings us to the final reason I think we should care deeply about aesthetics.

Quality is not just skin deep

As a final reason to care about and invest in the aesthetic design of your product, let me return to more abstract things. I started this chapter by suggesting that good aesthetic design would create for you a positive affect in your user — a beneficial frame of mind with which he would approach his first interaction with your product. I'd now like to suggest that such an impression could go deeper than that. I made the case earlier that such an effect/affect (both, in this case) is a genuine contributor to ease-of-use. It's harder to make that case for the effect I'm about to describe, which is why I've left it until last. I believe it's valuable nonetheless.

Software is, for the most part, a black box. With the exception of open source, and even then only for a few sufficiently skilled people, users cannot see what's going on "under the hood". And neither, as I've persistently asserted, should they have to. But if they can't see it, how will they know that it's any good?

Quality car makers have the same issue. None of their buyers will ever see the expense or excellence that goes into the design and manufacture of a complex and expensive gearbox, for example. Their solution? They make sure that the parts their users do interact with are of the highest quality, design and materials. That's why the steering wheel, gearstick, and most of all the key fob (which is almost the icon of the entire car), are beautifully designed and made. You can invite the same impression for your product.

Make sure that those parts of your product that your users interact with are well designed by making them simple and giving them a clear mental model. Make sure that those same parts are well made by incorporating high quality aesthetics. That way you will encourage your users to believe that those parts they can't see are just as well engineered.

If you do this, you'll give your users the impression that someone, somewhere in the team who created the product, actually **cared**. Of course, that assumption might not be true, but the reverse is surely true and users of products whose interactions are poorly designed are quite rightly entitled to assume that the hidden bits are just as bad. After all, you wouldn't spend a fortune developing a beautifully designed and engineered digital product only to scrimp, save, and under-deliver on the user-experience, would you?

Would you?

Summary

This has been the last of our three ways to improve the design of digital products. Over the last few pages, I've laid out a number of arguments to try to convince you of one thing: that how your product looks and feels really **matters**.

I've suggested:

- That first impressions count.   In other words, good aesthetic design puts your users in the right mood (we called it *affect*) for their up-coming experience of your product.   This might make them more tolerant of anything that doesn't work quite as it should, it might make them more likely to talk positively about your product with other people, and it may even make them willing to pay more for your product.

- That good aesthetic design supports simplicity.   It lets the **user** *see the wood for the trees*, and it forces **you** to think harder about reducing the number of features in your product.

- That good aesthetic design supports the mental model you've created.   It delivers and maintains the illusion, and it hides the real way the product works underneath. It also reinforces the mental model by providing appropriate feedback about what's happening.

- That a good test for whether something **works right** (for the user) is whether it **looks right**.   I talked about streamlined cars and the appeal of regularity and symmetry both aesthetically and functionally.

- That the aesthetic quality of your product is a key way that your users will judge the quality of what's going on where they can't see, under the covers.

Of course, great aesthetics are no substitute for a working product. Form without function is art, and that's not what I'm advocating here. But if your product works right, I believe you can help make it significantly easier-to-use by making it look right too. That is all.

Chapter 6

What now?

Over to you…

So that's it. I promised that I'd share with you three ways to make every digital product better. I said they wouldn't be a panacea, nor even hardly scratch the surface of the rich and multi-faceted disciplines involved in creating easy-to-use, valuable and desirable products. With the exception of what the product is **for** though, and most importantly **why** the user might want it (which is another story altogether, to say the least), I just wanted to share the three things I worry about more than nearly anything else whenever I'm involved in delivering new digital products.

In actual fact, what I've done over the last 100 or so pages — if it helps to think of it this way — is simply to offer you extended definitions of three adjectives that I think unarguably describe what easy-to-use digital products should be like, as follows:

sim·ple | ˈsimpəl| (1) Having a set of functions reduced to just those very most important functions that define the purpose and value of the product. (2) Free of all extraneous features, facilities and decoration.

in·tu·it·ive |inˈt(y)oōitiv| Embodying a mental model, inferable from the product's design, that provides a framework for reasoning about what the product does and how to use it, without reference to how it actually works.

de·light·ful |diˈlītfəl| Realised in a way that provokes in the user a positive aesthetic experience and response, prior to, and during product use.

That much is obvious. I've not shown you anything you didn't already know, really. After all, few people would argue that good products should be the opposite things: **complex, obscure,** and ***dreadful*** (my favourite antonym for *delight*ful). And yet too many products — software, gadgets, websites and machines that you and I have to use daily — are still exactly those three things. So perhaps what I've really done is just to encourage you to be more explicitly aware of these things, and to share with you some more objective reasons for why they matter, how they make a difference, and how to argue the case for investing in them with your colleagues.

These three ideas mesh tightly together — each supporting and amplifying the others. Another way to think of them is as layers, with the user's most immediate experience of the product at the top, his understanding of how it all fits together in the middle, and the product's actual functionality at the bottom. Like this:

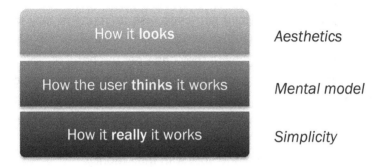

Whenever I find myself using a poorly-designed product, or worse, when I find myself trying to help someone else use a poorly-designed product, my overwhelming feeling is that nobody who worked on it **cared**. It is **not** hard to design easy-to-use products, and there are now more and more examples of great products that illustrate that possibility. But the poor products still outnumber the good by a huge margin, and the message I think the creators of those badly designed products send to their users is simply, *"we don't care about you"*.

If you've read this far (assuming you **have** read this far, and not just skipped ahead!), you can pat yourself on the back for caring. What you need to do next though — what you **must** do next — is to care enough to put these things into practice in the products you create.

At the beginning of this story, I suggested that us techies — by providing an unpaid support service — are keeping the purveyors of hard-to-understand products in business. But it's time to go on strike.

If you've ever helped someone else understand how to use the gadget they've just bought, or the software they've just installed, or the website they can't get the hang of, you'll know that there is a short-lived frisson of satisfaction to be had from being *the expert*. But I beg you to stop. Instead, help your family, friends and most importantly your business colleagues to understand **why** some products are easier-to-use, and persuade them to vote with their money.

None of us wants to put ourselves out of a role, but I can assure you that the satisfaction of creating a product that new users can use without any help, without reading the manual, and about which they say simply, *"It's so easy to use"*, outweighs and outlasts any momentary glow from being the best techie in the room.

Go on, make all our lives easier. Please?

Index

www.ingramcontent.com/pod-product-compliance
Lightning Source LLC
Chambersburg PA
CBHW052147070326
40689CB00050B/2421